TRAINSPOTTING DAYS

Silver Link Publishing Ltd

First published in 2006

British Library Cataloguing in Publication Data

A catalogue record for this book is available from the British Library.

ISBN 1 85794 267 1
ISBN 978 1 85794 267 5

Silver Link Publishing Ltd
The Trundle
Ringstead Road
Great Addington
Kettering
Northants NN14 4BW

Tel/Fax: 01536 330588
email: sales@nostalgiacollection.com
Website: www.nostalgiacollection.com

Printed and bound in Great Britain

Half title The classic trainspotter captured on the suburban platforms at King's Cross on Saturday 18 February 1967: short back and sides, school cap, hooded jerkin, short trousers, long socks, lace-ups, and duffel-bag complete with sewn-on badges. Into the notebook go a Brush Type 2 and a 'Baby Deltic'. The assortment of goods on the loaded platform barrows is another characteristic sight of the period. You will soon discover that nearly every picture in this book was taken on a Saturday, or sometimes Sunday – for obvious reasons, I suppose. *Frank Hornby*

Title page Grand National Day, Saturday 25 March 1961, has brought out the trainspotters on their bikes at Aintree – an accessible field at such a crossroads was irresistible. 'Black Five' No 45415 heads north with a Liverpool-Preston service, while above, at the Racecourse station, is a race special behind No 78061 and 'Royal Scot' No 46146 *The Rifle Brigade* – nearly all the 'Scots' were withdrawn the following year. 'Nicolaus Silver' won the race, at 28 to 1 – not that such mundane matters would have been of much interest to the spotters. *Peter Fitton, John Stretton collection*

Left The 'Brits' were among the most exciting and powerful-looking machines available to the mid-1960s spotter, and here No 70012 *John of Gaunt* (apparently minus its nameplates) stands at the north end of Lancaster Castle station with a Euston-Workington train on Saturday 9 October 1965, attracting the attention of all but one of the boys perched on the handy railing. Built in 1951, the loco is probably not much older than the spotters. *Gavin Morrison*

Right Ready for the off: a group of West Riding enthusiasts pose in front of their coach, possibly in Crewe in about 1952. Leslie Woolford, the gentleman in the second row below the sun-glare on the windscreen, organised shed-bashing excursions by bus on Sundays (when more locos would be on shed), including day trips to as far afield as Stranraer and Swindon – quite a journey by road in those days! They would probably see 1,000 locos in the day. *Gavin Morrison*

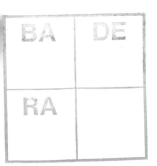

CONTENTS

FOREWORD
BY BRIAN BLESSED

When Will Adams asked me to write the Foreword for this wonderful book, I was absolutely delighted. Since my childhood in the early 1940s I have loved with a burning passion the sight of steam trains.

My home at the time was 30 Probert Avenue, Goldthorpe, near Rotherham, Yorkshire. The street was part of a circle containing a hundred houses or more. On opposite sides ran two railway lines – one was rusty and disused, but the other was part of the great London & North Eastern Railway. On many a summer's afternoon I would sit at the back of a neighbour's house that overlooked the LNER line, watching the smoking engines go by. Goods trains would be struggling with all their might to pull the wagons loaded with ore. Sparks flew as the wheels slipped, unable to grip the wet track, and the sweating fireman, lit up by the firebox, shovelled coal at an incredible rate in an attempt to sustain the engine. The roar of the frustrated locomotive and the massive eruptions of grey-black smoke from the chimney were reminiscent of some belaboured dragon, and inspired me to cheer them to the rooftops for their magnificent effort!

Brian Blessed with his daughter Rosalind (covered in grease!) pose in front of *Flying Scotsman* in 1992.
Brian Blessed

Left 'Cabbing' a loco was like being asked up on the stage at the panto – there were those who wouldn't dare put themselves forward, and those who were well up for it. Four spotters engage the fireman in conversation at Perth on Tuesday 22 June 1965 while the driver does a tour of inspection prior to working forward the 13.10 Aberdeen-Glasgow 'Grampian' express. Happily 'Streak' No 60009 *Union of South Africa* was saved from scrap the following year. *Ray Ruffell, Silver Link Publishing collection*

Moments like this were memorable, but nothing compared to the sight of the great express trains. Racing and pulsating across the countryside, these giants of iron and steel with their fiery bellies of burning coal sent shivers of pride through the hearts of all who beheld them. And what names they had – names that stirred the emotions, names that fired the heart and mind and evoked visions of misty dawns, red sunsets and promises of far-off and untold delights! *Green Arrow, Duke of Gloucester, Osprey, Princess Elizabeth, King Edward I, King Arthur, Lord Nelson...* Expresses like the 'Golden Arrow', 'Devon Belle', 'Capitals Limited', 'Queen of Scots', 'Royal Scot', 'Cheltenham Flyer' – not forgetting the pride of Wales, the magnificent 'Red Dragon', and the Southern's 'Bournemouth Belle'. Approaching that genteel seaside resort, the unmistakable sound of the latter's deep exhaust must have forced admiring glances from the reserved inhabitants and gladdened their hearts!

But what of Scotland, I hear you shout!

What the photographer describes as 'the glee of a "cop"' – 'A4' No 60021 *Wild Swan* (nicknamed 'Tame Duck' and numerically one short of the great *Mallard*) is the cause of celebration as it heads south through Doncaster station in 1961. It was withdrawn from service at the end of October 1963. *Malcolm Taylor*

Indeed! Scotland's voice was lyrical and loud in the early 1930s, demanding locomotives to challenge its fierce grades. In response, in May 1934, the famous 'Plant' Works at Doncaster produced the monstrous Class 'P2' No 2001 *Cock o' the North*. It was a massive engine, 73ft 8in long.

During the wild windy spring days of the late 1940s, youngsters like myself, with runny noses and streaming eyes, would gather at Doncaster 'Plant', and here we collected as many engine numbers as possible, and heard whispered tales of an apple-green locomotive that defied description and stupefied the mind! I am of course referring to the legendary *Flying Scotsman*. In a moment of fleeting lucidity, a young lad named Cedric whispered in my ear, 'It is the most stupendous engine ever created!'

'Amazing!'

'Stunning!'

'Breathtaking!'

'Gigantic!'

'When it thunders past yer, the whole railway embankment shakes beneath yer feet. If yer stand too close, it'll blast yer off yer feet!'

Bear with me, gallant readers, as I introduce to you Sir Nigel Gresley! A knight errant if ever there was one, he was appointed by the LNER as its Chief Mechanical Engineer from

A leaflet prepared by BR for a tour of Doncaster Locomotive Works on Wednesday 16 April 1952, providing a list of engines likely to be seen in and around the 'Plant' during the tour on that day. A guide was provided to escort the visitors. The note at the foot states: 'If you are nearing school leaving age and interested in railway employment the guide will be pleased to give you a British Railways recruitment form.'
David Holmes collection

its formation in 1923. He looked to Europe and homed in on the Italian racing-car – and railcar – manufacturer Ettore Bugatti. The combined talents of these two luminaries resulted in the LNER agreeing to the construction at Doncaster of a locomotive with the Bugatti wedge-shaped front. This ultimately led to – yes! – the smashing 'A4' 'Pacific' locomotives! Oh, I faint! I quiver! My, oh my! These great 'Pacifics' carried a variety of liveries – black, silver, grey, blue, green. Thirty-five of them were built at the 'Plant', from No 2509 *Silver Link* to the last, No 4903 *Peregrine*, and they were the most successful 'Pacifics' ever built. How do I know? Because, dear friend, I was there! There to see an express locomotive that tore out my innards and satisfied every mad craving in my imagination – I am of course referring to the greatest of them all, *Mallard*!

I saw *Mallard* at Doncaster half a dozen times, and on each occasion fell to my knees in supplication! I saw it burst through smog and rain, its colossal blue Bugatti wedge-shaped front powering through the weather, spraying water from the drenched track on to the train behind. The begrimed faces of the driver and fireman seemed suspended in a mist of volcanic red, swaying to the rhythm of the flying valve-gear. This devastating leviathan drove on like a blue Moby Dick, its fiery belly roaring out a challenge to the very elements! It is of course well known that on 3 July 1938 *Mallard* achieved a top speed of 126mph on a test run down Stoke bank, breaking the world speed record for a steam locomotive.

Sadly, during the summer of 1967 I sat on the embankment at Goldthorpe with my younger brother Alan and wept as the locomotives went by for the last time from far and wide. The powers that be had given orders for the remaining steam locomotives to report to various scrapyards throughout Britain. It was a holocaust of epic proportions. Like whales beached on distant shores, or elephants trumpeting from their secret burial grounds, the engines moaned and groaned as they fought to stay alive, until their last breaths hissed out and their great hearts ceased to beat.

Ladies and gentlemen, boys and girls, I really thought that was the end of the steam locomotive! Thank God it was not! They live! They live steaming through countries throughout the world, from the plains and mountains of India to the hot veldt of South Africa and the endless vistas of Russia and the Far East.

I am convinced that the photographs selected by Will Adams for this wonderful book will ensure that memories of those smoking dragons will live for ever! Congratulations, and much love to you all.

INTRODUCTION

'Is there any other means of transport ... which exercises so peculiar a fascination over young and old as the railway?'

Cecil J. Allen, *The Steel Highway*
(Longmans, Green & Co, 1928)

As I selected the pictures for inclusion in this book, I did so with a mixture of nostalgia and envy, of gratitude yet regret. For I have to confess at the outset that in trainspotting terms I was a late-comer, a child of the 1960s, and therefore caught only the declining years of the age of steam, which is the era that this book is mostly concerned with. How I envy those that were perhaps just five years older than me, who were shed-bashing in 1960 rather than 1965. And *ten* years older – well, although still or roughly the same generation, in railway terms they had known and experienced a distant, golden age of steam of which I can only dream through pictures like those included here. Yet what gratitude I feel at being a member of the very last generation to have known steam 'in the wild', for however good today's preserved lines are at 're-creating the past', they can never replicate *real*, everyday steam. For one thing, modern 'heritage railways' are in *colour*, while we all know that the *real* steam railway was in black and white – well, in my memory mainly sooty black and maroon.

Maroon because I was at first a prisoner in LMS-locked Coventry, and the brown and cream of the Great Western or the green of the Southern were lost to me. As a tiny child playing with my mother in the War Memorial Park beside the Coventry-Kenilworth line, I can recall seeing the crest of a locomotive's exhaust moving along the top of the cutting, and running for all I was worth towards the post-and-wire fence to catch a glimpse of the train itself below. Then, perhaps a little older, my first proper train-watching location was on an LMS line – *the* LMS line – the Trent Valley between Rugby and Brinklow near a farm called Cathiron, where there was a wide verge to park Dad's Ford Pop, and a footbridge spanning the four tracks. The shimmering lines stretched virtually straight in both directions, south-east to north-west, and the indistinct shape of a train could be seen approaching for a mile or more through the haze of a summer's afternoon. Then a Stanier 'Pacific' – 'shovelling white steam over her shoulder' as W. H. Auden put it – would explode from beneath the nearby road bridge and roar past. I could either watch from ground level, on the fence, or use the footbridge. Unfortunately I was too little to see over the solid parapets of the footbridge – painted in that coarse, sparkly grey paint that all bridges were coated with in those days – but I could hoist myself up on to the hand-rail to get a grandstand view.

Or should I say 'front circle' view, for train watching in the age of steam was pure theatre. Adrian Vaughan described his job as a signalman as 'probably the best job on the railway ... with a perfect view of the finest free show on earth'. Like the theatre, the steam railway was a world apart from everyday humdrum reality, full of noise and movement

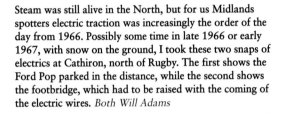

Steam was still alive in the North, but for us Midlands spotters electric traction was increasingly the order of the day from 1966. Possibly some time in late 1966 or early 1967, with snow on the ground, I took these two snaps of electrics at Cathiron, north of Rugby. The first shows the Ford Pop parked in the distance, while the second shows the footbridge, which had to be raised with the coming of the electric wires. *Both Will Adams*

and drama. What was seen from the fence or on the platform was totally different from anything else in life – absolutely nothing like a steam-hauled train could be experienced anywhere. Today, the railway seems to be at pains to make the experience as homogenous as possible – a station is just an open space, like any street in town, the trains are like cars, or buses, or planes. Then, signals, ingeniously and mechanically operated by a distant silhouetted figure in a signal box, told you what was about to happen, and where. Today the motionless signal shows clear regardless of whether a train is due in five minutes or five hours.

As a young trainspotter, you will remember the thrill of approaching a railway fence or bridge parapet and looking along the track, with its tidy foliage, neatly edged ballast and characteristic telegraph poles striding across the landscape, humming with messages or sighing in the wind. Better still was to visit a station. As in the theatre you had to buy a ticket, even if you weren't travelling. The usher/ticket collector barred your entrance to the auditorium, but once through and on to the platform you were in a new world. Lots of people used to work on stations, a large cast of

extras performing all manner of roles. A chorus of porters with long trains of solid-wheeled parcels barrows rumbling over the flags. The aforementioned signalman, the 'stage manager' of the production, pulling levers and changing the scenery with processions of passenger trains, long-distance and local, goods trains, shunting – remember shunting? – and much clanking and clanging and thumping and rumbling of assorted rolling-stock. Remember the syncopation of a loose-coupled goods train being brought to a halt in an echoing train shed, the disharmony of sound out of all proportion to the actual movement? Then how it all started again when the train was back on the move?

A level crossing was another great vantage point, when you could get as close to the 'stage' as possible. When we visited a great-aunt in Canley, I spent most of my day at Canley Gates, on the Coventry-Birmingham line. The road crossed the railway on a skew, so two very long gates sufficed, and passed each other in mid-travel. Because they were so long, the outer edge of each gate was travelling at high speed when the metal shoe on the bottom met the stop block by the roadside gatepost – the bottom of the gate stopped dead, but the upper part kept travelling, twisting the gate beyond its design specifications. The gates were always patched with metal straps in an effort to hold the woodwork together. Corporation buses trying to beat the gates were another cause of damage…

From those classical productions, those

Early electric days at Canley Gates, as the 11.15 Euston-Liverpool Lime Street passes on 24 August 1968, just a week or two after the total demise of steam on BR. I used to stand and watch the trains by the gatepost at the foot of the signal box steps on the extreme right. Today the crossing is no more, and the road is severed by the railway. *Michael Mensing*

Wagnerian operas, of yesteryear, with their rich scenery, fine costumes and Oxford English enunciation – 'The train now dyeparting from plyatform one...' – we've now got a kind of kitchen-sink drama in the round. Anyone – unless you're a camera-wielding trainspotter, of course – can wander in off the street, there's a cast of just one – if you're lucky – the scenery's minimalist, the music's dull and the plot's lost. It's cleaner, yes, more technologically advanced, faster, more comfortable – but where's the drama, the poetry?

The opportunity for a backstage tour – a shed bash – was irresistible. My grammar school had a Railway Society that organised coach trips to faraway places with strange-sounding names: Langwith, Doncaster, Royston, Normanton, Wakefield, Stourton, Neville Hill, Staveley – all visited during a trip to Leeds on 4 July 1965. I'd never been so far without my parents, and industrial Yorkshire was an entirely new landscape. Sheds were never located at the most salubrious end of town, and our coach would pull into some remote cobbled cul-de-sac and disgorge us through a gap in the sleeper fencing and down the fabled clinker path to the yard and shed – again, that wonderful sense of anticipation!

Sadly, number-collecting was a very competitive pastime at school, and to this day I regret that so much effort was spent in taking down every number we could clap eyes on, and so little was spent actually *looking* at the engines, the shed and the general railway environment, and no thought was given to *why* the engines were where they were, what they were doing and what the actual *business* of running the steam railway entailed. I guess we just thought the locos had been lined up by the staff for our collective convenience and entertainment. Row after row of those massive sleeping machines in the shed, the driving wheels towering above our little heads, the running-plates and boilers almost out of sight in the gloom. Gently sighing, small spouts of steaming water trickling onto the brick floor, or wheezing and squealing over the shed yard trackwork, heading who knew where. The sulphurous smell of new fires, getting the back of your throat, the soot and smuts, the inimitable smell of hot oil and steel, of steam. Never any thought for the poor souls who laboured in such places or on the locomotives prepared there. Just numbers, numbers and more numbers, the more 'cops' the better. At the end of the day, footsore, dirty and weary, you didn't care whether you ever saw another steam loco again. Now I have a right arm ready and waiting for anyone who could transport me back to those days (it's OK, I'm left-handed, so would still be able to scribble down the numbers...).

As I got older and steam got scarcer, groups of us would organise our own trips by train. A friend and I bought 'Runabout' tickets in the summer of 1966, and took ourselves all round the Midlands. By then there were more diesel and DMU numbers in our notebooks than steam, but the industrial landscape and the railway itself were still as fascinating a backdrop as they had always been, and the excitement was hardly diminished. This, of course, was in those innocent days before anoraks were derided, before palisade fencing was erected, before terrorists lurked behind every camera, and before paedophiles had been invented – and 14-year-old lads could safely take themselves off, courtesy of British Railways, to any sooty suburb they cared to visit.

We rarely had permits, of course – that would have been a bit too organised. But we found gaps in fences or handy back gates, and

managed to get round most sheds before the inevitable 'Oi!' resounded down the aisles of locos. We did no damage, we stole nothing, we sprayed graffiti on nothing, and we were tolerated, if not welcomed. Only once did we find ourselves 'on the carpet' – I can't remember where – to receive a mild talking-to from the shedmaster. (Sadly, my only criminal record stems from trainspotting – one day a group of us strayed inside the fence at the top of the embankment overlooking Coventry goods yard, and a passing zealous off-duty policeman took our names and addresses. I hadn't the wit to give a false one, and my parents duly received a visit from a bobby, and

One of our favourite haunts was 'the field' just south of Rugby Midland station. It lay in the angle of the junction between the Euston and Market Harborough lines, beneath the 'birdcage' bridge carrying the former Great Central line; the shed and testing station were just on the other side of the bridge. In this early 1960s view spotters make the most of the location, as a 'Brit', relegated to freight duties, heads south on the GC line. Today 'the field' is a modern housing development. *Iain Mackenzie*

Above My 1966 'Runabout' ticket – seven days' travel from Stafford to Northampton, Leicester to Cheltenham, for £1 1s 0d!

Right Day 1 of the 'Runabout' – a page of mainly diesels and electrics, with more steam encountered overleaf as we approached Shrewsbury shed, our first port of call.

I got another mild talking-to from parents who understood. The same goods yard provided me with my first footplate ride one evening, when, the forces of law and order being absent, a group of us were invited by the kindly crew of a Standard 4-6-0 – I think – to enjoy a ride from one end of a siding to the other. It was the first time I had experienced the effect of an engine's beat on the fire – awe-inspiring!)

For me and for all my fellow spotters, here was a hobby that was all-absorbing and highly educational. Even today my wide knowledge of UK geography stems from my early travels in search of engine numbers – if a place had a station or was near a railway, or had a loco named after it – then I'll have a fair idea of where it is. It is only in recent years, now that the world is oh so grown-up and sophisticated, that the hobby has become the object of ridicule. But I pity those who don't possess that basic human need to *collect* something, be it stamps, beer-mats, Victorian pot-lids, dolls, or engine numbers. I have several friends who bemoan their lack of a real hobby, and try and

invent ones for themselves – but it's not the same, and they come to nothing. It has to be *in* you, it has to evolve organically. I read that a Cambridge professor of psychiatry in a recent study claimed that trainspotters and other 'obsessive completists' were an extreme example of a general male fetish for compiling lists and studying systems, while the female brain is supposedly tuned to 'empathy' and 'social interaction'. Meanwhile, a Keele University professor claimed that 'Trainspotter' was one of 27 identifiable male personalities, including others such as 'Gadget Man' and 'Neanderthal'. Mmmm…

Whatever, I've no doubt that, for those with the right biological make-up, as soon as the first steam locomotive turned the first wheel *they* were there to start *collecting*. As soon as locos and trains could be photographed, the collectors were there collecting portraits of them. Perks, the porter in Edith Nesbit's *The Railway Children* of 1905/6, introduces Peter to the joys of number-collecting. I have a copy of *The Railway Book*, a highly illustrated children's volume published in 1925, which is dedicated to 'a four-year-old railwayist who never tires if the iron road and its steeds'. In May 1899 a self-styled 'railwayite', a Mr Bruce, pointed out that no organisation existed for 'that great and growing hobby afforded by railways', and as a result The Railway Club was founded; its first shed visit was to Nine Elms in November of that year. We have been branded 'railwayacs', 'locospotters', 'foamers', 'railfans', 'railbuffs', 'ferroequinologists' (proving that some of us 'students of the iron horse' had a classical education), 'anoraks' (about which the least said the better) and the mysterious 'gricers'. I once heard tell that this nickname arose from spotters' predilection for roaming the Cumbrian fells on the climb to Shap, when their only company was the grouse, or, if more than one, grice, presumably. Another theory is that trainspotting is somehow allied to grouse-shooting, bagging those elusive 'cops'. Quoted sources in dictionaries give the earliest recorded instances of the term in the late 1960s, but it's clearly older than that.

Serious organised trainspotting owes its origin to a man whose name has been synonymous with the hobby for more than 60 years, Ian Allan. 'I used to be a sort of spotter myself in the 1930s,' he told *The Railway Magazine* in 1999, 'although I never really wrote the numbers down – and there weren't any books in which to do so in those days anyway!' Which is where Ian Allan's fame lies. An enthusiast from an early age, as a teenager he began work as a temporary clerk in the General Manager's office of his beloved Southern Railway in July 1939, and soon became involved in the publicity department. He befriended the editor of the *Southern Railway Magazine*, who taught him the basics of what would become his great railway publishing empire. Because to everyone else the railway was 'just a job', any specialist enquiries from the public were passed on to Ian, especially those involving engines. He asked the chief clerk to supply him with a list of SR locos and shed allocations, then realised that demand for such information might justify a

published booklet. After some initial objection from 'upstairs', and despite the fact that 'there's a war on' and paper was short, the first cunningly-pocket-sized 16-page *ABC of Southern Locomotives* appeared in 1942. Apparently Bulleid was furious, but the SR Chairman congratulated the young clerk on his enterprise. Volumes on the other three 'Big Four' followed, publishing history was made, and locospotters had a new champion.

However, as related in Ian's autobiography, *Driven By Steam*, trouble was brewing. Lads gathered at good number-taking points in ever-increasing numbers, and at the railway crossroads of Tamworth as many as 200 boys might be seen congregating, some inevitably more irresponsibly minded than others. Placing pennies on the line landed some in Tamworth Juvenile Court, where the 'ABC' books were produced as evidence of this disturbing new movement 'sweeping the country', as the police

An early 'ABC' cover. *Roger Siviter collection*

A 1961 advert for Ian Allan 'abc' publications. *Ian Allan Publishing Ltd*

described it. Later, representatives of the constabulary toured schools warning of the dangers of messing about near or on railway lines. Ian Allan felt a sense of responsibility, and consequently formed the 'ABC Series Locomotive Spotters Club', later the famous 'Ian Allan Locospotters Club', designed to keep the growing army of spotters on the rails – or rather, off them. 'I undertake, on my honour,' swore each new member, 'not to trespass on Railway property nor hinder railway servants on duty and to endeavour to stop others from doing so.'

Ian Allan's stated 'raison d'etre' of the club (see – we trainspotters are conversant with Latin *and* French) '...is to further interest in locomotive and general railway matters. It is also to try to make enthusiasts realise that interest in engines is not merely a matter of number taking, but of something much more

fascinating and enthralling...' On the matter of responsible behaviour, the club booklet goes on: 'There are thousands of young chaps who play the game; but they are brought into a bad reputation by a relatively small number who think only of themselves and are a nuisance to everybody... We are very much in the Railways' debt for providing such magnificent entertainment for the price of a platform ticket.' Local groups were formed, pen friends sought, badges issued, rallies held, and models, books and stationery made available.

The familiar stereotypical trainspotter of the 1950s and '60s (and who continues to evolve today) was born. Whatever the hobby or pastime, there will be those who characterise the popular perception of the breed, and we're all lumped in together. 'You can spot them a mile away,' claimed Ian Allan in *The Railway Magazine* interview, knowing he had to tread carefully. 'They are totally over the top with their badges, beret, haversacks, notebooks, tape recorders, four cameras and the massive rows of ballpoint pens and badges they're festooned with. It's almost as though there's a trainspotters army,' continued their honorary Colonel-in-Chief. 'The more pens they have, the higher the rank they hold! ... Having said that, I don't agree with the press that spotting is a senseless occupation. So are a lot of other hobbies. What, for instance, does anyone get out of playing cards, fishing or walking round a field hitting a ball?' What indeed?

Ian Allan's own *Railway World* magazine reported on the 'Demise of the "gricer" – or let's preserve a railway enthusiast' in December 1969, in an article by the anonymous 'N. B. A.':

'Well, we've preserved nearly every moveable object (steam that is) on British Railways, but perhaps the greatest unpreserved loss has been the gricer, or full-time railway enthusiast. Illustrated alongside is the prototype design; note the particularly salient features of the species. Perhaps the most essential feature is the ankle-length gabardine mac; the "shortie" version is shown here. The sight of scores of these triffid-like figures sliding through

David Holmes's 1949 Ian Allan
Locospotters Club membership card.
David Holmes collection

GENERAL MEMBERSHIP

This is to certify that

D. Holmes

has been duly enrolled a
member of the
LOCOSPOTTERS' CLUB
as from 1 FEB 1949

GROUP MEMBERSHIP

The above is also elected
a member of the

GROUP L.S.C.

Initials of Secy.

SIGN THIS
DECLARATION
UNTIL YOU DO SO
THE CARD IS NOT
VALID

I UNDERTAKE, on my
honour, not to trespass
on Railway property nor
hinder railway servants
on duty and to endeavour
to stop others from doing
so.

(Signed) D. Holmes

MEMBERSHIP CARD

Name

D. HOLMES

No 26626

An account of an early Locospotters
Club 'invasion' of Swindon on
Thursday 1 September 1949, which
also included an air display at
Wroughton Airfield and an
opportunity to visit a local bus
garage! *Ian Allan Publishing Ltd*

Enthusiasts Invade Swindon

SPECIAL VISIT OF IAN ALLAN LOCOSPOTTERS

THE only unhappy person on the return trip of the special Locospotters' Excursion to Swindon Works on the 1st September was Maurice W. Earley who had been allocated a spot at Reading from which to take a photograph of the train as it sped through at about 80 miles per hour.

Unfortunately something went wrong. Adverse signals slowed down the train considerably, in consequence the driver shut off steam and down came a smoke pall over the train which was met by rising dust caused by the brake blocks being applied and at the critical moment the sun disappeared behind the heavy cloud. That is why the picture reproduced opposite is not quite up to Earley standard.

Apart from this everyone was in a happy mood.

The special train, consisting of 9 coaches and 3 kitchen cars, had left Paddington on time at 10.40 and the party arrived at Swindon at 12.12. Here, all had been conveyed in special " Bristol " buses to nearby Wroughton Airfield where the R.A.F. had staged a special display of aeronautics. This included special flights of jet aircraft which raced over the heads of 350

Spotters at well over 500 miles an hour, and made three engine drivers with the party—Messrs. Till ex-Southern Region, Porteous ex-G.W.R. and Earl ex-L.M.S.—hang their heads in shame for thinking that their 80 and 90 miles per hour were anything fast at all.

Then back again to Swindon for an extremely well organised visit to the Works, the highlight of which was No. 5018 on the rollers, that is the testing plant. It was going along about 50 miles an hour and yet it was standing quite still !

On leaving the Works the buses were waiting for the boys again and off they went to the local bus garage for further spotting and a thorough examination of the Bristol Company's buses at close quarters.

By 5.0 p.m., amazing to relate, everyone in the party and the guides were back on the train again ready for the fast run back to Paddington. The run was not quite as good as we had expected as you will see from Cecil J. Allen's accompanying Notes.

Luncheon and tea had been served *en route* and all and sundry, even the super-critics from Ian Allan Ltd., raised their proverbial hats to the Western Region for some really perfect organisation.

*   *   *

136

'The prototype railway enthusiast conforming in all details to specification… Many gricers were little different in design to the prototype.' The portrait illustrating the 1969 *Railway World* feature on 'Demise of the "gricer"'.
C. J. McBarr

binoculars, National Health spectacles and army surplus pack. The prototype's brain is powered by a computer which feeds instant useless information; this is then analysed and usually rejected by other computers of the same type. We are happy to report that some survivors are still at work and have been sighted on the Sussex borders recently; nevertheless we feel that for posterity one member of the class ought to be preserved before it is too late, perhaps to stand guard over the new York museum. Who will start the fund for donations?'

the fields of Shap in the rain will certainly be long remembered. Other features of the prototype include the inevitable cameras and tape recorder, with added luxuries such as multi-coloured ballpoint pens,

Happily, the author's report of the gricer's death was, like that of Mark Twain, an exaggeration. The infrastructure, the trains, the technology, the politics – everything, but *everything*, about the railway scene has changed since the 1960s, but the undying fascination with everything railway among people of a certain bent survives. The gricer is dead. Long live the gricer.

ACKNOWLEDGEMENTS

I would like to express my gratitude to all the many photographers who answered my call for 'trainspotter' photographs and searched through their collections to supply me with so many fine examples – without them, there would have been no book. If any reader happens to recognise himself in any of the photographs, please get in touch with me via the publisher! I gleaned many locomotive details from the very useful Rail UK website (www.railuk.co.uk). Geoff Body very kindly looked over the proofs, but any errors that remain are entirely mine. Finally, I must thank Brian Blessed for so enthusiastically supplying a Foreword for the book, the fee for which he asked to be donated to the Teesside Hedgehog Sanctuary.

1

PORTRAIT OF THE TRAINSPOTTER

When I started collecting pictures for this book it became clear that, for many photographers, the wandering trainspotter was an obstacle to the taking of a satisfactory record shot. Here's a case in point. In Crewe Works yard on Sunday 10 October 1948, in the early months of nationalisation, two veteran LMS locomotives were worthy of a photo but, as Ken says, the picture shows 'just how trainspotters can be so absorbed that they totally ignore the waiting photographer! I believe I could just about have throttled the clown who ruined what would have been an interesting picture.'
Ken Fairey

Happily for us, at the other end of the scale were deliberate portraits of spotters, which provide an invaluable record of the species in his (no women then) natural habitat. This unknown group is enjoying a visit to Bury shed on a sunny Sunday 8 April 1962. Note the variety of characteristic attire – duffel-coats, sports jackets, macs and blazers, flat caps and scarves, and stout footwear. The backdrop loco is Hughes 2-6-0 No 42730; their high-set angled cylinders and raised footplate earned the class the nickname 'Crabs' amongst enthusiasts.
John Stretton collection

Top John Chown and Bob Stelling have known one another since they started at junior school together in Tottenham in 1946. Both sent a selection of photographs from what John describes as 'those never to be forgotten days when we went out with the North London group of the Ian Allan Locospotters Club under the leadership of Jim Wyndham.' It was Jim who took the photographs. John continues, 'How I wish I could turn the clock back and relive those days once again. They were super times to me that will live in my memory until the day I die. I clearly remember going to visit Doncaster Works on a freezing cold New Year's Eve, but for the life of me I cannot remember the year.' The first photograph shows Bob (left), John (centre) and another spotter at King's Cross standing beside grubby 'A4' No 60014 *Silver Link* (appropriately!). This famous loco lasted until almost New Year's Eve 1962, being cut up at Doncaster the following January. *J. Wyndham, Bob Stelling collection*

Middle and bottom The year is very likely to have been 1949, as that was the year the nameplates seen here at Doncaster 'Plant' were applied to the appropriate members of the 'A1' Class. No 60162 *Saint Johnstoun* was numerically the last of the 50, completed in December 1949. The two 14-year-olds are seen with their mates carrying what today would be several hundred thousand pounds' worth of hardware! Bob is crouching in the centre and on the right beside *North Eastern,* and John at the back. *Both J. Wyndham, Bob Stelling collection*

Here's the gang again, probably on the same day judging by the weather. Some footplatemen have been encouraged to pose with the lads in front of an 'A4'. *J. Wyndham, Bob Stelling collection*

John Chown stands on the rail in front of 'Streak' No 60008 *Dwight D. Eisenhower*, formerly *Golden Shuttle*. Renamed in 1945, the locomotive was subsequently preserved and shipped to the USA. The location is King's Cross, and the date is Tuesday 14 August 1951. They're a mixed bunch sartorially, from baggy trousers to neat double-breasted sports jackets, and many appear to be wearing their Locospotters Club badges; the boy standing next to John has a belt with a 'snake' clasp, very characteristic of the era. *John Chown collection*

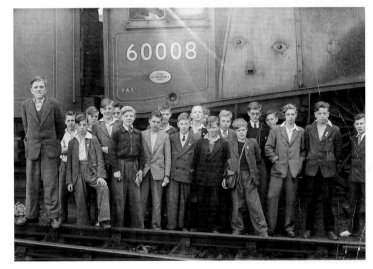

Much later, at Ferryhill shed, Aberdeen, on Friday 31 July 1959, trip organiser Jim Wyndham is seen (left) taking a photograph of the crew of preserved GNSR 4-4-0 No 49 *Gordon Highlander*. *Bob Stelling collection*

Left John, Bob and fellow enthusiasts are seen again on the footbridge steps at Stratford, east London, on Saturday 5 April 1952. *John Chown collection*

Bottom Another group are seen in front of veteran former GWR 'Bulldog' 4-4-0 No 3455 (originally 3744) *Skylark* of 1910. The location is unknown – possibly Oxford – and so is the date, although the last few 'Bulldogs' were scrapped by BR in 1951. *John Chown collection*

Right Somewhere on the Southern Region, 'Lord Nelson' 4-6-0 No 30860 *Lord Hawke* provides the backdrop for another delightful group portrait. Note again the widely varying styles of coats, macs and jackets. *John Chown collection*

Below right A rather more mature group from the Stephenson Locomotive Society's Midlands Area stands before the renowned *Flying Scotsman* during a visit to New England shed, Peterborough, in 1959. Left to right, they are Ray Rowley, Max Lock (visits organiser), John Dew, Lionel Bennett, David Johnson and Richard Mann. *Millbrook House Collection*

Below 'Jubilee' 4-6-0 No 45732 *Sanspareil* towers above a trio of spotters at Patricroft shed, Manchester, in 1962. 'We used to "do" the Manchester sheds as only Gorton

and Trafford Park locos regularly worked into Sheffield,' says Peter Denton. 'I took this picture because my father had just commented that he felt my mother did not realise how big "modern" locos actually were, of course only ever seeing them from platform level. When you look at the driving wheels set against my three pals (all of whom were of at least average height) you get an idea of the size of the beasts. The pal on the extreme right was still at school (we had by that time started work and were flushed with cash), and the other two worked for the railways, so he had in fact cycled all the way from Sheffield, hence his tight trousers with, I think, cycle clips holding them. Note the collar-and-tie attire of the other two.' Certainly the square-bottomed striped tie is very much of its era. *Peter H. Denton*

Right At about the same time Richard Derry was photographing a group of friends and fellow spotters at Cricklewood shed. He and his friends used to go on a London shed bash on a Sunday – '219 bus from home (Weybridge, Surrey) to Kingston, using a five-bob Red Rover ticket, then six sheds: Kentish Town, Camden, Cricklewood, Willesden, Old Oak Common, Neasden, and back to Kingston. During this visit to Cricklewood we got separated and I didn't believe the lads when they told me 46100 [*Royal Scot*] was on shed. Annoying, as I'd already seen 46100. Well, this photo proved me wrong.' Between the Thompson brothers on the left (one of whom is pointing to the loco) is Simon Lye, with a bag over his shoulder is Geoff Funnell, then Peter Walters and Ronald Matthews. 'Most of the lads were at school with me (not the Thompson brothers), and of course I've lost contact with all of them, most many years ago,' says Richard. *Richard Derry*

Right Part of a London itinerary from *The British Locomotive Shed Directory* of 1947 by R. S. Grimsley.

Neasden L.N.E. to Neasden L.P.T.B.
Leave the L.N.E.R. shed by the cinder path leading through the allotments to North Circular Road. On reaching North Circular Road turn right over the large railway bridge. The shed is in the L.P.T.B.

works, reached by a broad concrete path which runs from the left hand side just past the bridge.
Note.—Most of the lines in this vicinity are electrified.
Neasden L.P.T.B. to Cricklewood.
Return to North Circular Road, turn left, and walk a short distance to Neasden Lane. Board a south bound No. 16 bus at this point, and alight on reaching Edgware Road opposite the shed.
Cricklewood to Camden.
Board a Barnet bound No. 645 trolley bus outside the shed, and alight at Golders Green Station. Board a south bound Northern Line train to Chalk Farm Station. Cross the railway bridge (Regents Park Road) opposite the station, and bear left into Gloucester Road. Turn left into Dumpton Place, and the shed entrance is at the end of this cul-de-sac.

Reminiscent of those Victorian pictures with moustachioed company servants eager to be included and swarming over every available vantage point, so trainspotters couldn't resist the temptation to climb aboard a loco when the opportunity presented itself. Bob Stelling and his pals are on the running-plate of what appears to be a former LB&SCR 4-4-2 'Atlantic', bereft of its numberplate and nameplate. All six were based at Brighton, and the last, named *Beachy Head* by the SR, was withdrawn in 1958. *J. Wyndham, Bob Stelling collection*

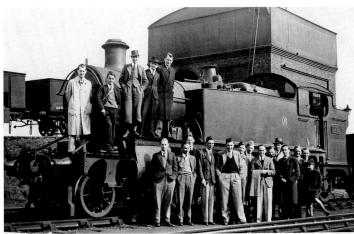

GWR 2-6-2T No 5134 provides the platform for a group of smartly dressed gentlemen at Leamington shed, possibly during the 1940s – the rather-too-small 'GWR' roundel on the tank side was introduced in 1934. *Peter Treloar, John Stretton collection*

The first outing of the Stevenage Locomotive Society on Saturday 30 May 1959 is marked by this artistic tableau of members on and around ex-LNER 'K3' No 61860 at its home shed at March (31B). Satchels are de rigueur, it would seem. The 'K3' was withdrawn and scrapped two and a half years later in November 1961. *Basil Coles*

It's July 1967, the Kinks' *Sunny Afternoon* is at No 1, and we're in the middle of the 'Summer of Love', although there's no sign here of the bead-wearing, pot-smoking love-in hippies that were so outraging decent society elsewhere – note the 'winkle-picker' shoes, 'drainpipe' trousers and elegant polo-neck shirts. At the south end of Carlisle's No 3 platform a group of enthusiasts chat with the driver of a 'Black Five' 4-6-0 – no trace of the number can be seen on the cabside – on a holiday relief train, probably from Glasgow to Blackpool. *Peter W. Robinson*

Above Notebooks at the ready, spotters cluster around 'M7' 0-4-4T No 30041 at what is thought to be platform 11 at Waterloo some time in the 1950s. The crew and the guard or inspector struggle to keep the job going despite the siege. *Raymond Percival, courtesy of David Percival*

There's an atmosphere of sad reverence as enthusiasts gather around 'West Country' Class No 34108 *Wincanton* heading the last BR steam train to Brighton in 1965. *Wincanton* was a last-minute substitute to take the train from London Victoria to the coast via Selhurst, and joined the train in a very filthy condition; some of the enthusiasts volunteered to clean it in the station, but they only managed to clean the nameplate. *Allan Mott*

Above Brake-vans were increasingly idle as freight trains fitted with continuous brakes became the norm, and they provided a novel vehicle for enthusiasts' specials, particularly with their open platforms. Here preserved ex-L&YR 'Pug' 0-4-0T No 51218 heads a Locomotive Club of Great Britain tour of the branches around Rochdale in the late 1960s. Is the gentleman in the first van recording the 'Pug' at work? *John Stretton collection*

Below Former Midland Railway 2F 0-6-0 No 58148, of an 1875 design rebuilt in 1917, performs a similar service at Desford for a Railway Correspondence & Travel Society (East Midlands Branch) tour on Saturday 12 May 1962. No 58148 was one of the last three survivors, and sister loco No 58182 was the last to go, in January 1964. *David Holmes*

Above Some years earlier, and somewhat more precariously, open wagons were provided for branch-line tours where passenger stock was no longer available. 'It is only real eccentrics who are prepared to travel along lines in open wagons,' recalls John Gilks of this trip on Sunday 9 September 1956, seen here loading at Whittlesea, east of Peterborough, for another RCTS trip, this time the 'Fenman' along the Benwick goods-only branch. The following week a picture in the local press bore the caption 'Slave trade at Whittlesea'! They later travelled on the Wisbech & Upwell Tramway in pouring rain. 'What the good residents of adjacent houses, obviously enjoying their Sunday dinners, must have thought of these mad foreigners standing in wet straw under their umbrellas defies belief. I can still remember the scent of damp clothing that pervaded the main-line train back to King's Cross.' *John Spencer Gilks*

Below Exactly five years later, in the days before 'risk assessment' had been invented, minimal protection and wooden planks for seats have been provided for the hardy enthusiasts on this special on the Denton Siding branch near Harlaxton, Lincolnshire, on Saturday 9 September 1961. No one seems unduly concerned, and a wife with bouffant hair-do and child are among the usually all-male contingent. *John Spencer Gilks*

Above On Sunday 29 October 1950 the Birmingham Locomotive Club chartered former GWR railcar No 14 from the city to Cheltenham, and it is seen here at Banbury. Macs predominate, the pre-war fashion for hats has not quite disappeared, and the gentleman on the extreme right is sporting 'plus-fours'. Well over 50 people can be seen here, so the 70-seater must have been well-filled. *John Edgington*

Below Twenty-four years later, on Saturday 30 March 1974, a coach outing connected with one of John Gilks's celebrated 'Talking of Train' courses pauses at Meldreth station, between Cambridge and Hitchin. The coach and the Moulton bike both date from the 1960s. *John Spencer Gilks*

Right A bicycle icon of the 1970s was the Raleigh 'Chopper', and John Gilks captured this trio of train-watchers using theirs to see over the concrete wall on to the Midland main line at Harlington on 3 June 1978. So that was what the characteristic long saddle was for...
John Spencer Gilks

Below and bottom The lure of the railway is as strong as ever, and it only takes a main-line special hauled by a steam loco or a classic diesel to bring out the crowds. The bridge parapet at Frosterley in the Wear Valley is just the right height for the gallery of photographers awaiting a North Eastern Railway Association special on 3 April 1993, but at Yeoford, in the heart of the Devon countryside, a good view of preserved diesel-hydraulic No 1015 *Western Champion* on 25 March 2003 requires the deployment of stepladders, which no serious railway photographer should be without! *John Edgington/David Mitchell*

Above One only has to compare these present-day views with those earlier in this section to prove that, while the 'gricer' is alive and well, fashions and technology have moved on. Casual wear and trainers are the order of the day – not a shirt and tie to be seen! – and the size of the camera-bags gives a clue to the kind of equipment the railway photographer carries around today. This group was photographed on the platform end at Chester in August 2004, and the less than exciting motive power is Class 47 No 47826 on a London-Holyhead service. *Paul Shannon*

Left and opposite page Ian Bishop supplied these three views of youngsters upholding the traditions of their trainspotting forefathers: a trio of cool dudes on an elderly seat at Nuneaton Trent Valley, binoculars proving handy for long-distance number-taking at Leeds, and a parcels trolley fulfilling its vital role as spotters' bench – although with the demise of Royal Mail by rail, are they already a thing of the past? *All Ian Bishop*

2
LINESIDE

To the dedicated lineside trainspotter – or train-watcher, for not everybody was or is taking numbers, but simply enjoying the scenic, aural and mechanical spectacle that is a living railway, especially in the steam age – vantage point is everything. A road parallel to the track, a footpath crossing, a lineside wall – anywhere suitable to sit and while away an afternoon by the railway, and of course somewhere firm on which to rest the notebook. These youngsters at Paignton have – to use that rather hackneyed but entirely suitable phrase – a 'grandstand view' of the south end of the station. The photographer recalls: 'Sometimes that wall was like a miniature stadium as it was crowded with shoulder-to-shoulder spotters, particularly on Saturdays. I even copped a Stanier "Jubilee" there.' The down 'Torbay Express' is departing on the last leg of its journey to Kingswear in August 1957. *Mike Morant*

Above These spotters have found themselves a couple of similar seats 'in the circle' on Tuesday 3 September 1963 to watch the drama of 'Castle' Class 4-6-0 No 5070 *Sir Daniel Gooch* assisting 'Warship' diesel-hydraulic No D831 *Monarch* away from Plymouth North Road with the 4.00pm train to Manchester/Glasgow, which includes a Travelling Post Office. *John S. Whiteley*

Below The access road to a goods shed at Apperley Bridge & Rawdon provides Dad (Grandad?) and the boys with a good view of passing 'Jubilee' No 45564 *New South Wales* with the 6.42am Saturdays-only Birmingham New Street-Glasgow St Enoch train at 10.51am on 25 August 1962. What looks like an Austin A35 Countryman would be worth spotting today! *David Holmes*

Above Flashback to an earlier 'Jubilee' age: on Wednesday 14 April 1948 at 5.45pm (after school) John Hargreaves photographed No 5711 *Courageous* on a Manchester-Glasgow express at Codley Bridge north of Preston. 'The spotter was my best friend Everard Flintoff,' recalls John, 'who later read Greats at Oxford and became a Senior Lecturer in Classics at York University until sadly he died. This was one of my very first dubious pictures on a Kodak folding Brownie, amazingly at 1/50th-second speed!' Nothing as substantial as this stout wooden fence would be seen beside our railway until the advent of today's supremely ugly palisade fencing. *J. E. Hargreaves*

Left This delightful photograph, captioned 'Daddy's train', is on the title page of *My Picture Book of Railways*, dating from the early 1930s. The two children – like something straight out of A. A. Milne – are perched on another substantial wooden fence to wave to what looks like a former Great Central tank on what I would guess is the GC&Met Joint line. *Author's collection*

Above Another 1930s view, this time at the north end of Stafford station on Sunday 25 March 1934, possibly on the occasion of an SLS shed visit. Spotters – including one who appears to be holding a bulky-looking camera – look on as another snaps 'Royal Scot' No 6109 *Royal Engineer* on a down express and 'Prince of Wales' No 5615 on a local. *Millbrook House Collection*

Right In a scene that could be from the 1930s – apart from loco number and livery – 'A4' No 60014 *Silver Link* (originally No 2509) is noted and photographed by bicycling spotters beside the East Coast Main Line at Hadley Wood on Saturday 1 September 1962 (five days before Little Eva's big transatlantic hit *The Loco-motion* entered the charts!). They were lucky, for less than four months later this pioneering locomotive would be withdrawn and ignominiously scrapped. *J. H. Bamsey, David Mitchell collection*

It's Sunday 11 February 1962, and electrification work on the West Coast Main Line has occasioned a diversion from the Trent Valley route on to the Aston-Stechford line at Ward End Park, Birmingham. This line would not usually see traffic other than freight, empty stock workings or diversions – the latter were quite frequent at this time, and have certainly brought out some local spotters to watch the unusual visitors. In the upper picture is English Electric Type 4 No D329 (later Class 40) with the 10.00am

Liverpool Lime Street to Euston train, while below is sister diesel-electric No D298 on the 10.15am Manchester Piccadilly-Stoke-Euston service. Very common in the Midlands at this time, these locos were 'Big Ds' to us, but were also known as 'Whistlers', from the very distinctive sound of their engines, which when I hear it takes me right back to pre-electrification Coventry! Note how the solid wooden fencing of old is now concrete posts and chain-link fencing. *Both Michael Mensing*

A few years earlier, on the late afternoon of Saturday 3 May 1958, Michael Mensing was photographing beside the line between Malvern Wells and Great Malvern. In the first picture the 4.25pm Hereford-Birmingham Snow Hill train is headed by 'Modified Hall' No 6984 *Owsden Hall*, while a little later '2800' Class 2-8-0 No 2864 climbed past with a down empty mineral train. The two boys were pupils at a nearby boarding-school and were taking a break from their studies on this sunny afternoon. There must have been countless thousands of miles of this post-and-wire fencing on BR, the wires kept spaced between the concrete posts by serrated bars held in place by clips. This stretch looks as if it may have been erected recently, as the wires usually became distorted and the bars dislodged – by spotters leaning and swinging on them, apart from anything else! Note also the wonderful telegraph posts and wires, a feature of the railway scene that was once so familiar, yet quietly disappeared without us realising it. *Both Michael Mensing*

Above Trespassing on the railway has always been strongly discouraged, and rightly so – the familiar threat of a fine 'not exceeding forty shillings' was literally cast in iron by the railway companies at countless crossings and access points. It's true that in years gone by trains weren't so fast and made a lot more noise, so it was slightly easier to avoid being killed or seriously injured, while in most places there was no threat of electrocution, and malicious damage was much less likely a motive, but that never justified getting on to the wrong side of the fence, as these spotters have near Aintree station on the former Cheshire Lines Committee route. On the same Grand National Day as the picture on the title page, Saturday 25 March 1961, 'Black Fives' Nos 44918 and 44667 bring in a race special from the East Midlands. The inspection cover housing on the cutting side makes an ideal platform! *Peter Fitton, John Stretton collection*

Below In much less clement weather in the dying days of steam, two spotters, well wrapped against the cold, watch as Standard 'Pacific' No 70010, formerly *Owen Glendower* but seemingly now minus its nameplate, approaches Shap with an up parcels train. The glory days of steam on Shap are long gone, and the 'Brit' is very grubby and not in the best condition, but in 1966 or 1967 the steam enthusiast had to make the best of what he could find. *John K. Morton, John Stretton collection*

Above As already mentioned, most railway photographers tried their best to keep enthusiasts out of their pictures, but the tousle-haired lad in the duffel-coat with his notebook and pen has just squeezed in on the extreme right, and has unwittingly become the focus of our picture. BR Standard 4MT 4-6-0 No 75047 is handsome enough as it waits to leave Wigan Wallgate with a stopping train for Liverpool Exchange in May 1965 – appropriately, No 1 in the charts that week was the Beatles' *Ticket to Ride*. The photographer recalls that this lineside fence was 'one of my favourite haunts of my youth, the street that runs parallel with Wigan Wallgate… Looking in the opposite direction trains on the West Coast Main Line could also be viewed.' *Tom Heavyside*

Right Magic Moments by Perry Como was at the top of the charts on Good Friday, 4 April 1958 (staying there for eight weeks), and a couple of lads are certainly enjoying one as former GWR No 4090 *Dorchester Castle* pounds away from Paddington past Old Oak Common with the 10.35am Paddington-Penzance express. I'm not particularly a Great Western fan, but the crisp four-cylinder beat of a GWR 4-6-0 at work certainly stirred the emotions! *Michael Baker*

Above More romantic and picturesque than a stone-capped brick wall is Letterston gorge in South West Wales, the ideal vantage point for a group of young trainspotters (some of the photographer's pupils, in fact!) to watch No 47134 as it takes the 09.18 boat train from London Paddington towards Fishguard on Tuesday 10 July 1984. *Paul Shannon*

Below In more recent years the comfortable, or at least tolerant, relationship between the railway and the outside world has deteriorated, and we are now shut out as much as possible. What was once a boarded accommodation crossing of the West Coast Main Line at Winwick Junction, north of Warrington, has been summarily severed, but it still provides a handy location for these cycling spotters. What we loosely used to refer to as a 'Peak', Class 45 No 45119, formerly D34 (much more romantic!), heads south on Wednesday 29 May 1985; it was withdrawn two years later in May 1987, and the now operationally extinct class was as lamented as many a steam loco. There's something almost Pavlovian about the human impulse to wave at passing trains... *Paul Shannon*

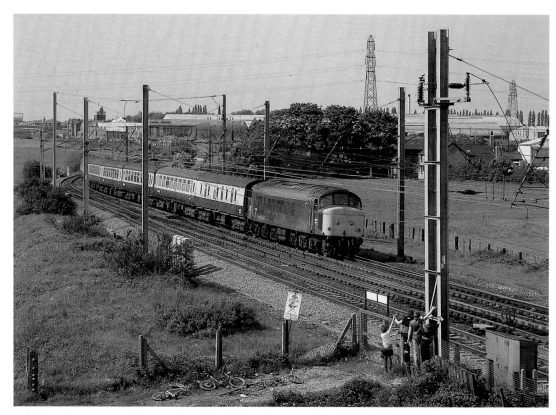

3
ALL STATIONS

Right Trainsheds acted as a resonator for all the sounds of the steam railway, amplifying the mechanical cacophony of locos and rolling-stock, the whistles of both locos and platform staff, station announcements, the rumble of solid-wheeled parcels trolleys... As a small boy I remember first experiencing the ear-bubbling shriek of a locomotive blowing off steam when standing roughly where this small boy is, in the north-end bay platforms at Rugby Midland, as it was then known. Through trains would approach relatively quietly from north and south, but once under that overall roof the fortissimo crescendo would roll round the station until the gradual diminuendo would become the pianissimo of escaping steam and tuneless railwaymen's whistling. On Saturday 27 June 1959, nine-year-old Fairburn 2-6-4T No 42062 has arrived at platform 3 with the 4.50pm from Leicester. The Leicester-Rugby line became the first of Rugby's branch lines to close, at the end of 1961, while No 42062 lasted until 1965 before withdrawal, less than 15 years old. *Michael Mensing*

Right There was always something happening at a main-line station. Schoolboy enthusiasts inspect the front end of ex-LMS 2-6-2T No 40050, standing beneath the Great Central girder bridge spanning Nottingham Midland station and waiting to leave with the 7.05pm Saturdays-only train to Worksop on 23 July 1960. Meanwhile another steam-hauled train stands in the up platform, and a new DMU occupies one of the through roads. The Fowler tank is in the last year of its life. *David Holmes*

Left Just occasionally in this collection a solitary enthusiast is seen in silent awe beside a locomotive. This delightful study shows a young schoolboy engrossed by the Walschaerts valve-gear of 'A2' 'Pacific' No 60504 *Mons Meg*, standing at Doncaster with an up semi-fast train for King's Cross while a member of the crew has a quick sweep round. Has man ever created a more graceful and harmonious motion than that of the eccentrics and rods of a Walschaerts gear in motion? *Les Nixon*

Below left Likewise attracting reverential gazes from young and old is former North British Railway 'J36' 0-6-0 No 65234, simmering beneath the great overall roof spanning one of the most exciting capital city stations of the steam age, Edinburgh Waverley. Remarkably, this 19th-century veteran survived until April 1967, long enough for me to see her in the summer of 1966 during a Scottish holiday. *David Hucknall*

Above right A few years earlier, on Monday 17 July 1961, three spotters are struck by the shining form of 'A4' No 60028 *Walter K. Whigham* as it stands in platform 10 at Waverley ready to take 'The Elizabethan' south towards the loco's home shed at King's Cross. For the three railwaymen, however, it's simply 'the office'. For enthusiasts named trains always had a certain cachet. 'The Elizabethan' was a 1953 renaming of the 'Capitals Limited'; the romance died when the name was dropped in 1963, the same year that the 'A4' was cut up at Doncaster. *John S. Whiteley*

Right With satchels and duffel-bags swinging, spotters soak in the activity and atmosphere at York, another great East Coast Main Line 'Mecca'.

The photographer remembers that in 1960 'this was an alternative trainspotting venue to Doncaster as there was a better chance of catching some of the Newcastle/Bristol trains as well as some North Eastern stock. I think this is what is happening here, with the "Pacific" ['A2' No 60539 *Bronzino*] coming off and being replaced by the "Jubilee" [No 45626 *Seychelles*]. I may be wrong but there might be an interesting tale to the date of this picture. It was, I believe, taken on the day of Princess Margaret's wedding to Antony Armstrong-Jones, and as we were given a day's holiday what better way to spend it than a trip to York – hence plenty of trainspotters. Years later I had the pleasure of meeting the later ennobled Lord Snowdon and I told him that thanks to him I had been given a day's holiday from school. There was little reaction.' *Peter H. Denton*

Above Because trains started, terminated or at least stopped at the larger main-line stations, they were an ideal place to catch a close-up view of the engine, and gaze longingly at the inner sanctum of the cab, with the fire's glare and the mysterious handles, levers and dials. If you stared long enough, perhaps a sympathetic footplateman might... Three hopefuls hover around the cab of smart-looking 'Britannia' No 70050 *Firth of Clyde* waiting to leave Glasgow Central station with the 4.30pm train to Liverpool Exchange and Manchester Victoria on 27 May 1961. *Michael Mensing*

Left There was less chance of cabbing a diesel – they had doors, and anyway time had moved on. The friendly face of English Electric Type 4 No D338, with its small, less disfiguring yellow warning panel, is seen at Carlisle at 4.30pm on a rainy Easter Sunday, 14 April 1963, working the down 'Royal Scot'. The enthusiast on the left is wearing smart black gloves and a scarf tied cravat-fashion. *John S. Whiteley*

Above Towards the end of steam, on Saturday 4 November 1967, preserved 'Streak' No 60019 *Bittern* takes water at Newcastle-upon-Tyne Central while heading an RCTS special from Leeds. Naturally a good number of enthusiasts have gathered, although something further down the line has caught the attention of one of them.
John K. Morton, John Stretton collection

Below Despite appearances, this photograph was taken more than five years earlier, on Saturday 2 June 1962. The 9.30am Glasgow Queen Street-King's Cross service is arriving behind eight-month-old 'Whistler' No D364.

The train was taken forward by sister loco No D244, and the 'fireman' is probably ready to jump down and uncouple. The number is being recorded by the lads on the right, seated on the traditional trainspotters' 'bench'!
Michael Mensing

Left An elderly sack barrow serves as a seat for these two spotters at York on another Saturday, 1 September 1962. D259 has arrived with the down King's Cross-Newcastle 'Northumbrian' – is another crew change taking place? *John S. Whiteley*

Below left There's just room for the spotter on the right to perch on the edge of the barrowful of mailbags while he records the number of 'Royal Scot' 4-6-0 No 46108 *Seaforth Highlander* at Birmingham New Street's platform 4 on a busy Saturday 19 September 1959. The train is the northbound 'Pines Express' from Bournemouth to Manchester (as the carriage roof-boards remind us), and the 'Scot' has probably just taken over from a Midland Division engine as usual. A steam-hauled Western Division train is approaching the spotters on platform 3. *Michael Mensing*

Above One of Michael Mensing's favourite photographic haunts in those days was Birmingham's other station, the former Great Western Snow Hill. On 5 August 1961 the three spotters seem staggered to be confronted with the relatively rare sight of an ex-GWR 'County', No 1002 *County of Berks*, running in with the 9.45am Paddington-Wrexham train. These relatively unsuccessful 4-6-0s were all withdrawn between 1962 and 1964. The nearest boy wears a school cap and mac, shorts, ankle-socks and lace-ups. Note also the approaching elderly lady with her cases, brolly and 'flowerpot' hat. *Michael Mensing*

Below Seen from the other main through platform, 'Hall' 4-6-0 No 4912 *Berrington Hall* arrives with what is probably the 9.02am Margate-Wolverhampton Low Level service. It's 5.49pm on a busy holiday Saturday, 9 August 1958, and Michael noted that the train was 2½ hours late. The spotters on the left won't mind, as long as the day brings lots of 'cops'. *Michael Mensing*

While two boys hover around the cab end of 'Castle' Class No 5070 *Sir Daniel Gooch* on the 11.10am Paddington-Birkenhead service at Snow Hill, another, in school uniform and long socks against the cold, studies the front end on Saturday 23 November 1957. Nearer the 'commercial' end of the train, the Guard stands with hands clasped behind his back. Properly paved platform surfaces are now a thing of the past. Too expensive? Potentially too slippery? Too many joints to trip on? To big a risk of litigation? *Michael Mensing*

Above The shape of things to come: an elegant eight-car 'Blue Pullman' diesel-electric multiple unit set calls at Snow Hill forming the 4.50pm Paddington-Wolverhampton 'Birmingham Pullman' on Monday 9 April 1962 (coincidentally Brunel's 156th birthday), during 'Western Railway Week'. The service had begun the previous year, and lasted until March 1967, providing a fast service to and from the capital at a time when the West Coast Main Line was severely disrupted by electrification works. The elegance of the front end, complete with Pullman crest, is certainly capturing the attention of the spotter in the duffel-coat and his mate, not to mention the enthusiast-to-be (perhaps) in his (her?) father's arms. Michael comments that 'the nearest lad on the right, quite unknown to me at the time, about a dozen years later identified himself when I spent several years working alongside him!' *Michael Mensing*

Below A bobble-hatted spotter and his little friend compare notes having taken the numbers of Brush Type 4 No D1699, at the head of the 1.10pm Paddington-Chester General train, and light engine English Electric Type 4 No D226 at Snow Hill on Saturday 1 October 1966. The 'Big Ds' (later Class 40) were common in the Midlands, and I have all the namers from D210 *Empress of Britain* to D235 *Apapa* underlined in my 1965 Ian Allan 'Combine'! *Michael Mensing*

Above The 'Cambrian Coast Express' was introduced by the GWR in 1927, running from Paddington to Aberystwyth/Pwllheli. Re-introduced by BR in 1951, it ceased in 1967, came back in 1987 as a Euston-Aberystwyth service, then disappeared finally in 1991. In its heyday as a BR express, the down train calls at Snow Hill on Saturday 2 December 1961 behind Old Oak Common's 'King' Class No 6021 *King Richard II*. A bunch of hopefuls stand politely beside the cab, while Dad and the boys keep a respectful distance. No 6021

was cut up just over a year later, at Cashmore's of Newport, at the age of 32½, just six months younger than its Royal namesake, who died in February 1400 aged 33 (I thought it was about time we had a useless fact). *Michael Mensing*

Below Six months earlier, in June 1961, Malcolm Taylor captured the train at Shrewsbury, running in behind 'Hall' 4-6-0 No 7928 *Wolf Hall*. Again, the spotters have obviously been waiting for it. *Malcolm Taylor*

Above This afternoon Dad has brought the boys to Dudley Port Low Level station on the former LNWR Wednesbury-Dudley line, and watches on as the lads scribble down the number of ex-LMS 8F 2-8-0 No 48514 rumbling through with a southbound freight at 5.49pm on Saturday 25 July 1959. The wonderful symphony of sound created by a rake of assorted loose-coupled goods wagons was one of the joys of the steam railway, the different wheelbase lengths, shapes and loads bringing their own sounds, together with the occasional squealing flanges, catching brake-block or clanging buffers, the rhythm continuing long after the engine's own sounds had faded. Behind the group is a poster advertising the film *South Pacific*, then on release. If that's too exotic, next to that is a poster advertising Skegness... *Michael Mensing*

Below On their way home from Skegness are the passengers on board this Butlin's holiday express, heading south through Hitchin station just after 3pm on Saturday 28 June 1958; the locomotive is 'B1' No 61113. Hitchin was one of those favoured stations with a loco shed adjacent to the station (Cambridge was another), and the combination of a shed 'visit' ('B17/4' 'Footballer' No 61653 *Huddersfield Town*, withdrawn in 1960, is visible) and a busy Summer Saturday East Coast Main Line location has attracted at least 17 spotters. The photographer and his fiancée had travelled over the line from Bedford for the afternoon; that line closed on New Year's Day 1962, and the 'B1' fared a little better, being withdrawn from Lincoln shed in September 1963.
J. E. Hargreaves

Above What may be another Saturday holiday train calls at Oxford General on 8 August 1964; perhaps Leeds Holbeck's 'Jubilee' No 45562 *Alberta* is returning holidaymakers from the South Coast to Yorkshire. Once again a young spotter stares reverentially at the footplate – a steam loco's cab was a unique environment with its own special sounds and smells. No wonder we all wanted to be engine drivers when we grew up! *J. H. Bamsey, David Mitchell collection*

Below At 10.40am on Saturday 12 May 1951 another 'Jubilee', No 45580 *Burma*, gets away from Preston in an eruption of smoke and steam at the head of a Liverpool-Glasgow express. That same day, on the other side of the world in the Pacific Ocean, the first H-bomb test produced an eruption of an altogether different kind… The photographer reckons that the schoolboy spotters are most probably from one of the local grammar schools at Preston, Kirkham or Lytham St Annes – Preston was a favourite weekend spotters' venue for miles around, he tells us. *J. E. Hargreaves*

Right Leeds was another important railway centre with several main-line stations/termini and a good number of sheds – Holbeck, Stourton, Farnley Junction, Copley Hill and Neville Hill – all accessible by foot or tram from Leeds City station. City grew from Wellington (LMS) and New (LMS/LNER) stations, linked together in 1938, while next door was Central, also jointly operated by the two companies. Central closed and the other two were rebuilt as one in 1967. At City in August 1958 a spotter is captured in animated mood beside 'B1' No 61238 *Leslie Runciman* and another unidentified loco. He is wearing a shirt and tie, shorts and a school blazer, with his mac over his arm – an adult in miniature. But in 1958, the year of Cliff Richard's debut hit and Elvis's *Jailhouse Rock*, teenagers were only in their early prototype form. *Mike Mitchell*

Right Another double-header at the west end of City: at 4.36pm on a sunny Saturday afternoon, 5 September 1959, 2-6-4T No 80116 leads 'A2' 'Pacific' No 60539 *Bronzino* on the 2.20pm Liverpool-Newcastle train. Once again spotters have made themselves at home on barrows and whatever the structure in the foreground is. *David Holmes*

Left Next door at Leeds Central ex-LNER 'J39/2' 0-6-0 No 64886 has just arrived with the 11.15am relief from Fleetwood at 2.50pm on Saturday 12 August 1961. The photographer has captioned the picture: 'Small boy to driver with pipe: "I'd like to be a driver when I grow up."' *David Holmes*

Above It looks like a chilly Good Friday, 20 April 1962, and in this delightful portrait the two spotters are well wrapped up in their macs and long socks on the platform at Cardiff General. One of them writes down the number of '5600' Class 0-6-2T No 6682 as it crawls towards adverse signals with an up coal train, trip 'H14'. It looks as though the fireman has taken the opportunity to operate the injectors. *Michael Mensing*

Below More number-taking is under way at St Pancras on a wet Saturday 21 January 1961. With 2 minutes to go, No D227 awaits departure with the 1.55pm service to Manchester Piccadilly. 'Jubilee' No 45641 *Sandwich* can be glimpsed at the adjacent platform. *Michael Mensing*

Right When there was still steam to spot, diesel multiple units were beneath contempt, and in this scene at the south end of Derby on Saturday 23 May 1964 spotters young and old turn their back on a Nottingham-bound example to note the number of 'Black Five' No 45236, approaching with an excursion that has probably originated from the Birmingham or Bristol area, although Sheffield and other Midland trains over the Peak District main line also ran that way into Derby. The track is the one that was used by through trains, which used to creep through at walking pace. In front of one of Derby's roundhouses stands Standard 2MT 2-6-0 No 78000, built at Derby and often seen there, so probably shedded locally. *John Hilton*

Below In 1964 the idea of writing down DMU carriage numbers would have seemed absurd, but by 1979 you had to collect what you could find. The first spotter thumbs a lift from the driver of Set C596, comprising Class 119 and 101 units (now dubbed 'Heritage' units in an attempt to give them some nostalgic dignity), as it arrives at Severn Tunnel Junction as the 17.55 Cardiff Central-Bristol Temple Meads service on 29 September; he's in danger of being struck by the prematurely opened door. Long trousers, hooded anoraks and a flight-bag have replaced the school uniforms and duffel-bags of old. *Michael Mensing*

Above Spotters galore have descended on Spalding station on Saturday 8 May 1976. The town's famous Flower Parade has attracted many excursions, including 'Hastings' units 1036 and 1037, which have just arrived from their 'home town'. It's clearly lunchtime, and some postal trolleys have been adopted as dining area and cloakroom. From the flight-bag on the trolley has emerged a plastic sandwich-box, bottle of squash, and something in a bowl. The baggy trousers and large shoes of the boy with his back to us have a distinctly 'Bay City Rollers era' feel about them (although on this Saturday *Fernando* by Abba reached No 1, remaining there for four weeks). *Roland Hummerston*

Below The 'Deltics' carried a steam-age allure into the diesel age and were deservedly sought out and admired by enthusiasts. All in anoraks, jeans and trainers, these three consider the bulk of No 55015 (more romantically the former D9015) *Tulyar*, happily now preserved. It is standing at Darlington at 10.35 on Thursday 27 October 1977 with the 08.00 Edinburgh-King's Cross service. The all-over BR blue livery with large yellow warning panels was nowhere near as attractive as the original two-tone green. *David Holmes*

Top While the 'Deltics' had a stern, rather heavy-featured 'face', I always felt that the 'Peaks', with their smaller noses, looked very friendly – dolphins rather than whales, perhaps? Like the 'Deltics' they were much lamented when they finally all disappeared towards the end of the 1980s, except for the fair number that survived in preservation. No 46022 (the former D159) was sadly not one of them, and there's much flicking of number-books as it stands at Bristol Temple Meads on Saturday 27 March 1976. Rucksacks and flight-bags are much in evidence, including one from BOAC, which had become part of British Airways two years previously. *John Hillmer*

Middle No 46039 (D176) is seen broadside-on at Manchester Victoria on Wednesday 10 June 1981 flanked by spotters in characteristic poses – sitting on a trolley and leaning on a surviving roof column. Beyond is Class 40 No 40104 (D304). *John Hillmer*

Bottom Tuesday 15 May 1979 was clearly clement enough to allow a couple of these young spotters to lie on the warm flagstones and one to discard his shirt as they watch No 45019 (D33) pass with a parcels train along the down fast line at Tiverton Junction. Albeit slightly dilapidated, the steam age infrastructure of buildings and lower-quadrant signals survives to enhance the view. Tiverton Junction was replaced by Tiverton Parkway on a different site almost exactly seven years later, on 15 May 1986, and No 45019 was cut up at Vic Berry's yard that October. *Tom Heavyside*

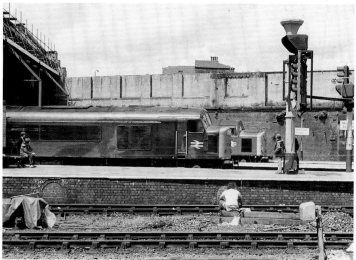

4
THE PLATFORM END

Left Having explored the body of the station, we now move to the platform end. The fact that by far the majority of pictures submitted for use in this book were taken at this location indicates how important it was as a spotting venue. For it was here that the locomotive was normally to be found, and you could either just stand and stare or, if you were lucky, get yourself invited on to the footplate. As the crew of 'Castle' Class No 5003 *Lulworth Castle* busy themselves prior to departure south from Bristol Temple Meads, one lad is already on the cab steps, with others eager to follow. The letter 'C' could then be written beside the engine number in your *ABC*! *H. G. Usmar, David Hucknall collection*

Below left More cabbing activity is under way at London's Liverpool Street terminus on Saturday 20 September 1958. 'Britannia' No 70013 *Oliver Cromwell* is at the head of the 3.45pm express to Clacton; at least one boy is already on board and blocking access, while another has grabbed the rails and seems intent on pushing his mate on! At the smokebox end two other boys are studying the cylinder, while a teenage boy and girl, the latter in tartan trews, walk casually away. Beyond, six or seven spotters have sat

themselves down on the platform ramp, with a panoramic view of the station throat. *Frank Hornby*

Above Across town at Euston, on Saturday 13 July 1963, the fireman of gleaming 'Duchess' 'Pacific' No 46345 *City of London* is engaged in conversation by a trio of spotters as the loco blows off ready to depart with the 11.40am 'Lakes Express', the summer service to Windermere/ Keswick and Workington. Gerry and the Pacemakers are topping the charts with *I Like It*, and we're definitely in the era of tight-fitting jeans with turned-up bottoms. To my mind – born into the LMS stronghold of Coventry – Stanier's 'Pacifics' are arguably the most handsome locomotives ever to run on Britain's railways. Discuss. Sadly, by the end of 1964 this example had been reduced to scrap. *Frank Hornby*

Below At the end of one of the arrival platforms at Euston in 1954 two smartly dressed young gentlemen watch the arrival of 'Jubilee' No 45606 *Falkland Islands*. As at Liverpool Street (opposite) another couple of boys are sitting on the platform ramp. *H. P. White, Allan Mott collection*

Above In about 1955, down the Euston Road at St Pancras, with its distinctive gas-holders, another 'Jubilee' is arriving, much to the excitement of the school-capped spotters. This time it is No *45610 Gold Coast*, which was updated by British Railways to *Ghana* after independence and a change of name in 1957. Thus railways not only provided a good practical geography lesson, but also a lesson in international politics! *Frank Hornby*

Below Across the river at Waterloo, 'air-smoothed' Bulleid 'Merchant Navy' Pacific No 21C14 (BR number 35014) *Nederland Line* waits for the midday departure time of the down 'Devon Belle' to Ilfracombe on an unknown date (although the train only ran between 1947 and 1954, and the loco is in its original SR guise, so probably earlier than later). The spotter on the left has had quite a severe 'short back and sides'! *Mike Morant*

'And at this end are the smokebox and cylinders...' Getting in some early education in steam loco matters is a smartly dressed Dad and his young son in check shorts and sandals. The subject of the lesson is 'Battle of Britain' 'Pacific' No 34087 *145 Squadron*, waiting to leave with a boat train for Southampton on Tuesday 16 May 1967. In a few weeks, on 10 July, the last scheduled steam-hauled train would leave Waterloo, and such daily sights would be the stuff of history. *Les Nixon*

As Dad explains the niceties of Bulleid's design philosophy to Mum, their son is more interested in the fireman clambering on to the tender, perhaps prior to taking water at Basingstoke on Monday 22 May 1961. The engine is 'Merchant Navy' No 35012 *United States Lines*, as modified with the 'air-smoothed' casing removed and Walschaerts valve-gear added, a process that began in 1956. Beyond, the fireman of Standard 4-6-0 No 73110 *The Red Knight* is likewise busy aloft, before working forward a Bournemouth express from the Eastern Region. *Michael Baker*

At Southampton West, beneath its famous signal gantry, 'West Country' 'Pacific' No 34024 *Tamar Valley* takes water as a spotter looks on. The others are grown-up enthusiasts, the nearer armed with briefcase and brolly rather than duffel-bag and notebook. The train is probably a Waterloo-Bournemouth West/ Weymouth service. *J. W. Armstrong Trust*

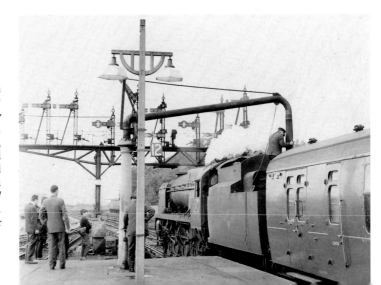

Above Clapham Junction is 'Britain's busiest railway station', and has thus always been a spotters' favourite. In 1952 the 'little and large' sight of 'Lord Nelson' 4-6-0 No 30863 *Lord Rodney* piloted by 'H' Class 0-4-4T No 31320 has set the enthusiasts running, young and old alike. In the background is the junction's famous 'A' signal box, of an LSWR design and dating from 1905. The tank is only two years younger, and lasted until 1955. *The late N. L. Browne, Frank Hornby collection*

Below Here's *Nederland Line* again, this time with its BR number on the smokebox door and powering through Clapham Junction some time in the early 1950s on a down express. The lone spotter is about to be enveloped in that heady cocktail of speed, sound and smoke. *Mike Morant*

Opposite above Some 25 years later 'A' signal box has lost its canopy and been rebuilt, and the main lines west

from Waterloo have lost their steam. On Thursday 10 August 1978 five spotters at the platform end note down the number of 4-VEP unit No 7710 – not quite as exciting as a 'Merchant Navy' in full flight, but needs must. The four boys sitting in the foreground, who are not old enough to have seen steam at work on the Southern, are engrossed in conversation. *Frank Hornby*

Below In the early 1990s the signalling centre at Wimbledon took over responsibility for Clapham Junction and the signal box was closed and demolished. The relatively less interesting vista from the platform end has not deterred modern-day enthusiasts, however, and a group of more mature spotters – the lads above grown up? – congregate as of old on Friday 30 October 1998 as Class 412 4-BEP No 2304 arrives forming the 13.00 Waterloo-Portsmouth Harbour service. Their bags are ever larger and more sophisticated, mirroring their contents; a biro and notebook are no longer enough in the digital age! *Brian Morrison*

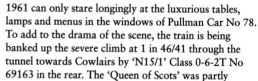

Above Moving to the other end of the country, the sight of 'A4' No 60031 *Golden Plover* leaving Glasgow Queen Street with the up 'Queen of Scots' Pullman for Edinburgh and King's Cross is an exercise in pure elegance. This is what railways are supposed to look like, and the boys on the platform end on Saturday 13 May 1961 can only stare longingly at the luxurious tables, lamps and menus in the windows of Pullman Car No 78. To add to the drama of the scene, the train is being banked up the severe climb at 1 in 46/41 through the tunnel towards Cowlairs by 'N15/1' Class 0-6-2T No 69163 in the rear. The 'Queen of Scots' was partly replaced by the 'White Rose' Pullman in 1964, and *Golden Plover* was withdrawn and scrapped at the end of 1965. *Michael Mensing*

Left 'Oh, no – just a pair of ugly unreliable diesels. What happened to steam?' bemoans the spotter on the right as he and his friends walk disconsolately away from North British Type 2 diesel-electrics Nos D6135 and D6108 on the 12 noon train from Glasgow Buchanan Street to Oban on the same day. Introduced in 1959, these short-lived locos had all gone before the introduction of the TOPS numbering scheme, most well before the last in 1971. Nonetheless, the wonderful array of semaphore signals rescues the scene. *Michael Mensing*

Above Trainers, T-shirts and expensive cameras characterise these modern-day English spotters at the platform end at Glasgow Central on Thursday 29 August 1996, as Class 318 No 318267 arrives leading the 16.33 service from Ardrossan Harbour; the route indicator has already been set for the next part of the diagram, to Ayr. In no way does the train or the scene compare with that opposite, but at least it's still a living, busy railway. *Brian Morrison*

Right Thirty years earlier, at 8.30am on Saturday 18 June 1966, a platform-end quartet watch as 'B1' 4-6-0 No 61263 prepares to leave Perth with southbound empty coaching stock. White trousers and shoes were never the wisest dress in the vicinity of a steam locomotive...
Roger Siviter ARPS

Above Carlisle Citadel station was an exciting melting-pot of many railway companies from north and south of the border, and was still a Mecca for trainspotters well into the BR era, as seen here on Saturday 5 September 1959, with former LMS and LNER steam locos flanking an English Electric Type 4 – what wouldn't we give to be transported back to such a scene? On the left is 'Jubilee' No 45729 *Furious*, then, beyond the 'Whistler', 'Black Five' No 45029 and 'A3' No 60096 *Papyrus* on the up 'Waverley', bound for St Pancras via the Settle & Carlisle route; this train had been so named in 1957. Presumably some engine-changing is taking place, hence the locos on the centre roads. *Mike Mitchell*

Below No 45029 and another locomotive are now apparently at the head of the 'Waverley', and in place of the Type 4 is sister 'Black Five' No 45395 with another up train. All this activity added such interest and spectacle to the business of number-collecting in the steam age. *Mike Mitchell*

Right On the other side of the country the following summer, at Newcastle-upon-Tyne Central on Saturday 2 July 1960, another LNER 'Pacific' runs in, no doubt much to the pleasure of the spotters assembled on the platform end. It has just traversed the famous diamond crossing in front of the castle, which can be glimpsed above the cab. Gateshead shed's 'A1' No 60150 *Willbrook* is at the head of the 9.50am Aberdeen-York train.

R. Leslie, courtesy of
J. W. Armstrong Trust

Below A paper carrier-bag with string handles (remember them?) is an unusual spotter's bag, but is the choice of the young gentleman in the centre of this group gathered at the business end of the up platform at Grantham in about 1949. 'A2' 'Pacific' *Sayajirao* still carries its LNER-style number E530, but has the early-style 'BRITISH RAILWAYS' on the tender; it would shortly become No 60530. Built and named in March 1948, the previous year the loco's namesake racehorse had won the St Leger, the same year that Tudor Minstrel and Pearl Diver (fellow 'A2s' Nos 528 and 529) won the 2,000 Guineas and Derby respectively. But I bet none of the lads knew how 'Sayajirao' was pronounced – does anyone? *J. F. Clay, John Stretton collection*

Above At the north end of York station was – and still is – the junction of the East Coast Main Line swinging away to the north-west and the Scarborough line to the north-east. Ranged along an assortment of benches and barrows at the end of the very long main up platform are more than 15 spotters revelling in the sight of 'A3' No 60111 *Enterprise* arriving during August 1959, just ten years before a rather more advanced *Enterprise* – NCC-1701 – arrived on our TV screens from America! Home-grown TV science-fiction in 1959 was the BBC's famous series *Quatermass and the Pit. Mike Mitchell*

Below Three years later, Type 4 No D396 is seen at the same place with an up Anglo-Scottish car-carrier. BR began the first long-distance overnight car service between King's Cross and Perth in 1955, and this daytime service followed in 1960, between Holloway and Edinburgh and return. Again there are in excess of 15 spotters on the down platform. *John S. Whiteley*

Above Looking into the station from the north end, 'Streak' No 60030 *Golden Fleece* is seen departing with a down express around 1960, watched by spotters on both sides of the line. In the background rises the bulk of the Station Hotel of 1852, still one of the city's premier hotels, though now in private ownership. *John S. Whiteley*

Below At the same platform York shed's 'V2' 2-6-2 gets under way with a down troop train on 10 September 1960. The usual Saturday crowd of more than 20 spotters has colonised some barrows in the time-honoured way. *R. Leslie, courtesy of J. W. Armstrong Trust*

Above On the London Midland Region in the Midlands in the early to mid-1960s, the 'Brits' were about the most exciting steam locos on offer – their smoke deflectors distinctly branded them as express engines, and their high running-plates meant that the wondrous motion of the Walschaerts gear was well exposed. And of course, they were all – bar one – named. At Preston on Saturday 19 June 1965 No 70020 *Mercury* (sans nameplate) is about to erupt into life with an express for the south. Half a dozen spotters seem to have formed an orderly queue in the hope of 'cabbing' the loco, but the fireman is studiously ignoring them. The 'Pacific' lasted another 18 months before withdrawal in January 1967. *Ray Ruffell, Silver Link Publishing collection*

Below At Sheffield Victoria on Saturday 9 July 1960 No 70037 *Hereward the Wake* waits to leave with the Harwich boat train. Peter Denton remembers: 'During school holidays a real treat was to visit Victoria, the prime reason being to catch the Liverpool-Harwich Parkeston Quay boat train. It had been pulled from Manchester by an EM2 electric loco, then that came off and usually a Norwich loco came on, as in this case. Sometimes it was a "B17", but in this case I recall taking the picture because any "Pacific" loco in Sheffield was something of a rarity – and I had a soft spot for them. I even took my sister trainspotting here on occasions but not always accompanied by my trusty Kodak Brownie box camera.' *Peter H. Denton*

Right Another Norwich 'Brit' was No 70013 *Oliver Cromwell*, seen here with its 'proud owner' (according to the photographer's caption!) at Leicester Central on Saturday 23 July 1960. It moved from Norwich to Carlisle Kingmoor in 1963, and became the last BR-owned steam loco to undergo a routine heavy overhaul at Crewe in 1967. At Carlisle it saw out the demise of steam in Britain, being one of the locos that hauled the famous 'Fifteen Guinea Special' to mark that sad event. It was then preserved as part of the National Collection in preference to No 70000 *Britannia*, which was subsequently sold privately. At the time of writing it is undergoing overhaul to bring it back to main-line standard. On 1 November 1965 I saw No 70054 *Dornoch Firth* crossing the 'Birdcage' bridge at Rugby (see page 13), the last steam loco I saw on the GC line – by September 1966 it had closed as a through route to the south. *Mike Mitchell*

Below The 'B1s' were also regular performers on the former Great Central line, especially before its transfer from the Eastern Region to the London Midland Region in 1958. On Saturday 8 March of that year, two spotters scribble down '61008', named *Kudu*, as it waits to leave Nottingham Victoria for Marylebone with the up 'South Yorkshireman'; introduced in 1948, this express was withdrawn in 1960, along with others on the line, marking the beginning of the end for that splendidly engineered route. Beyond, at the up slow platform, is a 'J39' 0-6-0. *Mike Mitchell*

Above Down below at Nottingham Midland, the main St Pancras line was a regular stamping ground for 'Jubilees', and here we see No 45627 *Sierra Leone* resting at the east end of the station on Saturday 31 May 1958. A spotter in a smart leather(-look?) jacket and his friend hover around the cab, but the fireman is taking a no doubt well-earned rest with his right boot up on the window-sill. The BR 'lion and wheel' emblem on the tender was a very elegant device, by contrast with the 'double arrow' logo that followed, which was terribly modern but very dreary. *Frank Hornby*

Left A rather grubbier 'Jube' – No 45618 *New Hebrides* – is seen taking water at Chinley at 10.21am on Saturday 28 February 1959 while taking a 'Footex' football special from Luton to Blackpool. Why aren't the group posing in front of the cab wearing replica soccer shirts…? This season 'the Hatters' had already seen off Leeds, Leicester and Ipswich in the FA Cup, and the quarter-final replay against Blackpool on 4 March saw a record crowd at Kenilworth Road of more than 30,000. They beat Norwich in the semis to meet Nottingham Forest in the Final, but lost 2-1. From then on a steady decline set in, until a revival in the mid-1960s. Meanwhile, over in the East of England the Midland & Great Northern Railway system lost its passenger services on this day. *Basil Coles*

Above Two spotters squatting on the platform end at Leeds City on Sunday 1 July 1962 are the filling in a tasty sandwich formed by ex-LMS 'Mogul' No 43124 on the 2.18pm Bradford Forster Square train and 'Peak' No D106 with the 1.58pm Bradford-Derby service. Unusually, the 'Peak' has a steam-type shedplate on its nose, indicating that it is Derby-based. *John S. Whiteley*

Below The previous year, on Saturday 5 August 1961, 'J6' 0-6-0 No 64203 receives instruction at Leeds Central. Platform-end trolleys once again provide the enthusiasts with seats, and someone has thoughtfully provided a solid, though sloping, writing surface on the one on the right! *David Holmes*

Above Knots of spotters, together with a couple of parents by the look of it, congregate at the platform end at Manchester London Road on Saturday 3 September 1955 – some are even sitting on the bench provided! Apparently not of any great interest is veteran former Great Central 'C14' 4-4-2T No 67445 of 1907.
H. C. Casserley, John Stretton collection

Below Just five years later we're into the diesel and electric era at London Road. It's Saturday 9 April 1960, just five months before the station was renamed Piccadilly – electrification work is taking place in the background, and new colour light signals are being installed to replace the fine LNWR examples in the foreground. In the bright spring sunshine 'Whistler' No D236 is reversing the empty stock of the up 'Lancastrian' into platform 4, watched by a dozen or more spotters on the handy platform 'peninsula'. *Michael Mensing*

Above Across the city at Victoria station, it's Saturday 1 June 1968, in the last few months of everyday steam on British Railways. A group of spotters watch ex-LMS 8F No 48369 run tender-first into the east end of the station while engaging in some shunting. *Roger Siviter ARPS*

Below We're now standing on the same platform as the spotters, and another tender-first loco – one of only two named 'Black Fives', No 45156 *Ayrshire Yeomanry* – approaches from the Manchester loop at East Junction with empty stock. Fellow 4-6-0 No 45203 has a parcels van in tow on the left. *Roger Siviter ARPS*

Above The scene is now Liverpool Lime Street, and at 4.09pm on Good Friday, 31 March 1961 ('typical Bank Holiday weather!' notes the photographer wryly), 'Jinty' 0-6-0T No 47519 reverses the empty stock from the 10.10am from Euston back into the station; new overhead catenary gantries are being erected ready for electric services the following year. Two duffel-coats, a school mac and a donkey-jacket are keeping the worst of the rain off the four spotters watching the operation. *Michael Mensing*

Left Ten years later, on Tuesday 24 August 1971, a solitary spotter is apparently hoping for something a bit more inspiring than No E3166, waiting at the head of the 14.30 Euston service. At least the driver's a bit more cheery than the old fellow on the 'Jinty' – must be the better weather... The electric still has its raised numbers on the cabside, a touch of style on otherwise slab-sided locos that some enthusiasts dubbed 'Cans'. *Ray Ruffell, Silver Link Publishing collection*

Top Unchained melody! At 2.11pm on Saturday 18 June 1955, in the week that Jimmy Young topped the charts with his first big hit, the up 'Royal Scot' approaches Wigan North Western, with Stanier 'Pacific' No 46254 *City of Stoke on Trent* wearing the famous headboard. The sight and sound of such an express rushing through the station is enough to tempt a young spotter to step tentatively forward on the down platform. Lucky lad! *David Holmes*

Middle 'Kilroy was here'? The cheekiest of the knot of spotters leaves his mark on 'Black Five' No 44860 while the driver's attention is occupied by the business of departing from Stockport Edgeley (just plain Stockport after 1968) with a down express at 5.04pm on Saturday 9 April 1960. *Michael Mensing*

Bottom A year later, on Saturday 4 March 1961, Michael Mensing captured this conversation piece at Stafford, with D318 calling with the 11.45am Euston-Crewe train. The two older enthusiasts are engaging the driver in conversation while the younger boys, both with duffel-bags, compare notes. As can be seen from the scaffolding on the up platform, not much of the original station above platform level remained at this date. It had been demolished in preparation for rebuilding in connection with electrification; however, a question-mark hung over the whole grand Modernisation Plan at this time, due to the parlous financial state of the British Transport Commission. The wires were eventually energised here in 1963/64. *Michael Mensing*

'Please can we go on the footplate, mister?' However, the fireman in the beret doesn't seem able to oblige in this undated but clearly pre-electrification view of the west end of the Midland side of Birmingham's New Street station. The 'Jubilee' (Bristol-shedded so probably en route to that city) is No 45577 *Bengal*, while former Midland Railway 2P 4-4-0 No 40511, from nearby Saltley, is on pilot duty. *Millbrook House Collection*

Above Running into platform 7 in the Midland section of the station from the south-west, and going into the notebook, is 'Jubilee' No 45651 *Shovell* with the up (northbound) 'Devonian' from Torquay and Paignton to Leeds and Bradford (platforms 1 to 6 were the 'North Western' side and 7 to 11 the 'Midland'). Descending into the station behind the retaining wall is Queen's Drive, which split the site in two. The date is Saturday 29 April 1961. *Michael Mensing*

Right A fortnight earlier, on the 15th, entering New Street from the west on the North Western side is 'Black Five' No 45387, passing 'New St No 5' signal box with the 12.15pm from Blackpool. Being below street level, the station was surrounded on all sides by tall retaining walls, and crossed by massive girder bridges. As the photographer notes, 'The two nearer boys seem to have found me more interesting than the engine!' The others are busy getting the engine number down. *Michael Mensing*

Above Forward again to 29 April 1961, leaving platform 5 is 'Britannia' 'Pacific' No 70021 *Morning Star* with the empty stock of the 12.14pm arrival from Watford Junction, watched from platform 6 by an assortment of travellers and spotters. I doubt that so many would take such an interest in a departure today, within the gloomy cavern that is the modern overbuilt New Street. 'Brit' '21 almost made it through to the end, being withdrawn on New Year's Eve 1967. Note the height of the buildings forming the northern 'cliff-face' above the station, being the rear of the station's Queen's Hotel in Stephenson Street; a replacement was not included in the rebuilding of 1963 in connection with electrification, and it closed it doors on New Year's Eve 1965. *Michael Mensing*

Below We now move to the east or London end of the station, and at platform 7 on the Midland side is rebuilt 'Royal Scot' No 46137 *The Prince of Wales's Volunteers (South Lancashire)*; it is Saturday 1 July 1961, and Diana Spencer, the future wife of the man who would be the next Prince of Wales, is being born in Sandringham. The train is the 10.05am Bournemouth West to Derby. In the absence of the usually ubiquitous platform barrows, the traveller has resorted to sitting on his suitcase, while the spotter on the right has had to lean his notebook on his leg. The gabled buildings fronting onto Worcester Street rise above the entrance to the tunnel that takes the lines down then up to Proof House Junction on a 1 in 58/51 switchback. *Michael Mensing*

Above Approaching platform 6 on the North Western side is Rugby's 'Black Five' No 44771 with the 7.02am from Yarmouth Vauxhall on Sunday 29 October 1961. Beyond it, on platforms 4/5, are some spotters around the base of the curious totem-pole-like semaphore signal; all its works are 'inverted' at the top of the post to avoid damage to passengers or spotters, and its main arm is cut short due to the restricted width. Beyond again is another 'Black Five' at platform 3. *Michael Mensing*

Right At the same point a few years earlier, on Friday 26 April 1957, another Stanier 4-6-0, No 44872, arrives with the empty stock to form the 6.00pm departure to Manchester London Road. Having finished school for the week, the well-wrapped-up schoolboy contemplates the 'Black Five'. *Michael Mensing*

Above Not far away was Birmingham's former Great Western station at Snow Hill. As at New Street, the lines at the south-eastern end of the station plunged into a long tunnel towards Moor Street on a falling 1 in 45 gradient. Emerging from the gloom of the tunnel at the top of the gradient at 2.51pm on Saturday 4 July 1959 is '5700' Class 0-6-0PT No 8737 with a down freight. Picked out in the afternoon sunlight at the end of the up platform are two spotters, one in a cable-stitch sleeveless jumper with his shirt sleeves rolled up – his father in miniature! The other lad looks a little cooler (in both senses) in a short-sleeved T-shirt. *Michael Mensing*

Below A fortnight later, at just after 2 o'clock on 18 July, and also taking a down freight along the through line between the platforms at Snow Hill, is '5600' 0-6-2T No 6667, being studiously recorded by the quartet of spotters. *Michael Mensing*

Above By contrast, the north-western end of the station was airy, the line emerging onto a viaduct as it left the city centre. On Saturday 9 July 1960 'King' No 6027 *King Richard I* pulls away with the 2.10pm Paddington-Birkenhead Woodside express down the 1 in 47 towards Hockley. No barrows to sit on, but an iron railing is available for leaning while notes are compared. In April 1962 Peter Handford was on the GWR main line at Hatton recording No 6027 pounding up the bank with a Birmingham-bound express; released by Argo Transacord on the LP *The Great Western* in 1966, it remains one of the most impressive and exciting recordings of a 'King' – or any steam loco, for that matter – hard at work. *Michael Mensing*

Below On the up side of the station in the late-afternoon sun, four enthusiasts watch 'Modified Hall' No 7908 *Henshall Hall* shunting parcels vans in platform 10 at half past 5 on Saturday afternoon, 18 July 1959. In the background is Taylor & Challen Ltd, makers of power presses. Interestingly, the firm still exists today as part of power press spares and service company TMA Engineering Ltd, which has a railway maintenance arm whose customers include Midland Metro, current occupiers of today's re-opened Snow Hill station, as well as several preserved railways. Great Western lower-quadrant signals were among the most elegant and distinctive of all, especially when most other companies converted to upper-quadrant. *Michael Mensing*

Below From July sun to driving February sleet mixed with steam, which is obscuring most of Rugby Midland's great trainshed. Braving the elements at the west end of the station are two enthusiasts; presumably it was worth a soaking to see side by side sister 'Jubilees' Nos 45726 *Vindictive* and 45703 *Thunderer* – appropriately violent names for this wintry Saturday, 22 February 1958. The train at the platform is the 12 noon Euston-Crewe. The photographer notes that 'spotters were often a nuisance when they got in the way, but without them the Rugby Midland print would have been pointless!' Rugby was a great trainspotting venue; its good-quality buffet was centrally placed on the huge island platform, with doors to both up and down sides for quick exits to catch numbers of through trains. *Mike Mitchell*

Bottom As mentioned in the Introduction, my home town is Coventry, but I don't really remember the pre-electrification station, which was demolished and rebuilt, and re-opened on 25 May 1962. On 19 April 1958 Ivatt 2MT 2-6-2T No 41320, a Northampton loco, leaves the station with the 1.20pm Nuneaton Trent Valley-Leamington Spa Avenue train, the kind of train I would have seen running past the Memorial Park at about this time. The service was withdrawn in January 1965, but with the opening of Birmingham International station, between Coventry and New Street, many trains bound for the South and West now call at Coventry and take the Leamington line rather than the more direct former GWR route from Birmingham. The spotter would be a couple of years older than me – I wonder if I knew him. *Michael Mensing*

Above The former GWR line through Leamington headed south to Banbury, where this photograph was taken on Saturday 25 August 1960. The clock in front of the loco reads 2.16pm, as 'Black Five' No 44825 restarts an up part-fitted freight after taking water. The two spotters have nothing to do on this summer afternoon but listen to the bark of the 4-6-0 as it gets under way. Another point for discussion: surely the two- or four-cylinder 'four beats to the bar' rhythm is more satisfying than the over-hurried 'six beats to the bar' of a three-cylinder engine, or is it just that I was brought up in LMS rather than LNER or Southern territory? Just look at those wonderfully graceful semaphores! *Michael Mensing*

Above right Further south again is Oxford, where the sight of Standard 9F 2-10-0 No 92001 is exciting considerable interest at the main down platform on Saturday 7 August 1965 – although either the photographer or something happening behind him is also turning heads. Steam was increasing rare at this time – Oxford shed closed in January 1966, and the 9F, a Tyseley engine at this time, was withdrawn from Wakefield on its 13th birthday, 31 January 1967, and scrapped the following May. *J. H. Bamsey, David Mitchell collection*

Left Iconic or unique locomotives have always been a draw. This portrait of the sole BR 8P 'Pacific' No 71000 *Duke of Gloucester* heading north from Crewe with 'The Mid-day Scot' was taken with a box camera in July 1954 when it was only a few weeks into service. Its name arises from the fact that HRH the Duke of Gloucester was Honorary President of the International Railway Congress held in London on 19-26 May 1954. My 1960 *Observer's Book of Railway Locomotives of Britain* observes, 'Unfortunately, owing to the decision to cease construction of steam locomotives, no more of this class will now appear.' The eager enthusiast wasn't to know that it would be withdrawn just 8 years later – or that it would still be running on the main line more than 50 years later. *Alan Fozard*

Below Twenty-five years later, in July 1979, Brush No 47105, the former D1693, enters Crewe from the south with a down Freightliner. Rather less iconic for sure, but the venue still attracts a good clutch of spotters, a platform barrow is available as ever as a seat, and a flight-bag and flask are still doing sterling service. *John Hillmer*

Above Although one of a class of 30 'Kings', the GWR's 'flagship' loco No 6000 *King George V* was unique in carrying a brass bell presented to it when it visited the Baltimore & Ohio Railroad's centenary celebrations in 1927. While farewells are exchanged further down the train, spotters – one with classic school-cap and duffel-bag – prefer to stay close to this most elegant of express locomotives as it stands at Bristol Temple Meads on an unknown date. Withdrawn in 1962, No 6000 is now part of the National Collection. *John Stretton collection*

Below The 'Black Fives' of the diesel era, the Class 47s were – and the survivors still are – reliable workhorses. On Saturday 7 February 1976 No 47096 (which entered service as D1682) goes in the book at Taunton as it leaves with the 10.23 Manchester Piccadilly-Plymouth train. The old platform barrow has been replaced as a seat by the more 'high-tech' equipment cabinet! *Tom Heavyside*

Above From their introduction in 1961, despite being early interlopers in the still-steam-dominated express passenger business, the 'Deltics' were recognised as a race apart. Their imposing design, deep throaty roar and unsurpassed speed and power marked them as worthy of the enthusiasts' attention, and certainly the dozen spotters at the south end of Doncaster station on Saturday 18 April 1964 will not have disdained to write the number of D9018 *Ballymoss* in their notebooks. Allocated to Finsbury Park for most of its 20-year career, it was named at Doncaster on 24 November 1961, the day it was delivered (Ballymoss having won the town's St Leger horse race in 1957). Withdrawn in October 1981, it was cut up at Doncaster the following January. *David Hucknall*

Left A bonus for West Coast Main Line spotters was the period between 17 March and 20 August 1979 when the East Coast route was blocked by the partial collapse of Penmanshiel Tunnel, and Edinburgh services were diverted via Carstairs and Carlisle. Away from its usual stamping-ground, *Ballymoss* is seen again, by now renumbered 55018 and in the less than flattering BR Corporate Blue livery, leaving the north end of Carlisle's platform 3 in August 1979. *Peter W. Robinson*

Above No 55014 *The Duke of Wellington's Regiment* (the former D9014) leaves an exhaust haze over King's Cross as it sets off for Edinburgh on a wet day in October 1981. Perhaps the spotters have braved the weather knowing that a month later the locomotive would be withdrawn from service, and by February 1982 would be scrap-metal at Doncaster Works. *Michael Baker*

Right Another relatively short-lived class of powerful diesels that gained a dedicated following among enthusiasts was Class 50. Introduced on the West Coast Main Line in 1968, the 'Hoovers' – so-named because their engine note resembled that of a domestic vacuum cleaner – later found themselves on the Western Region, where No 50008 *Thunderer* (which started life as D408 in March 1968) is seen at Exeter St Davids on Tuesday 28 August 1984 with the 09.32 Penzance-Paddington service. The last of a long line of locos to carry this name, from a Liverpool &

Manchester 0-4-2 in 1836 via the 'Jubilee' seen on page 86, it was withdrawn in June 1992 but survives in preservation. *Roger Siviter ARPS*

Above Wet weather has never been a deterrent to the dedicated spotter. Hooded against the wet, this group of enthusiasts are at Guide Bridge station on Monday 9 July 1979, recording the passage of Class 40 No 40193 with a train of tanks and hoppers. Introduced as D393 in June 1962, it only lasted until October 1981, when it was withdrawn; however, nearly five years were to pass before it was cut up at Swindon Works. *Paul Shannon*

Below Our final platform-end view is again in the wet, on a rainy May Bank Holiday at Gatwick Airport station on Monday 28 May 1984, the 26th anniversary of the station's opening in 1958 and the day that Eric Morecambe died. Class 47/4 No 47445 (the original D1561 of March 1964) passes with the 09.58 Manchester Piccadilly-Brighton train. Trainers, jeans and casual jackets characterise the modern spotter – a world away from the shorts, blazers and caps of old! *Brian Morrison*

5
INTERLUDE: SCHOOL OUTING

Right When John Fenning was teaching at a school in Bath in the early 1960s, he took the boys on several trainspotting trips, and although the dates and itineraries are now lost in the mists of time, the photographs he took evoke the era of such trips, when school uniform was obligatory and orderly behaviour a must! The first photograph shows the group assembled at Bath Spa station. The *Observer* poster is advertising 'Man Without God' by eminent biologist Sir Julian Huxley. He was commissioned by the *Observer* to write a series of articles for the paper in 1960, and one entitled 'Science and God' appeared in *The Observer Weekend Review* on Sunday 17 July 1960 – so there's a good chance that was the day that the week of excursions began. (If any readers recognise themselves, please get in touch!)

All photos by Rev John E. Fenning

Below The first day saw the party in London, and here they are taking a break courtesy of the familiar parcels barrow at the old Euston station. This ramshackle collection of assorted platforms of inadequate length was totally rebuilt in 1963-68. Nine Elms was also visited that day.

Above On Monday they went south-west, and this picture was taken at Exeter St Davids shed. Under the watchful eye of a railwayman they approach a 'Castle' Class 4-6-0 – the number looks like 5020, which was *Tremanton Castle*. Note the typical assortment of bags being carried.

Left They were at Plymouth in time to see the 'Cornish Riviera Express'. Note the very organised boy in the centre with his clipboard!

Left On Wednesday they went north, and here are some of the boys on the train at Bristol Temple Meads at 8.15am. It looks as though they had reserved compartments.

Above One of the Wednesday ports of call was Shrewsbury. A china cup and saucer from the buffet for your tea – those were the days!

Above right South Wales was the destination for Friday, and 0-4-0ST No 1338 was sufficiently rare to be the subject of this photograph at Swansea East Dock. The last of its class to survive, and the last surviving former Cardiff Railway locomotive, it had been built by Kitson in 1893. It saw out its last days shunting in the Swansea area.

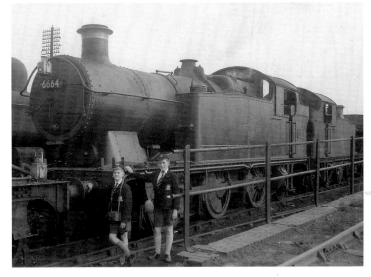

Right '6600' Class 0-6-2T No 6664 was a 1927 Collett design for the Welsh Valleys, and was photographed at Pontypool Road.

Below The repair shops at Carmarthen were another Friday visit. One wouldn't have thought that white shirts and school uniform were ideal attire in such close proximity to steam locos!

Above left Other outings were also photographed. In this delightful portrait you can almost smell the dusty well-sprung moquette seats!

Above The gang, some looking a little weary, are seen here during a trip to Derby.

Left A line of diesel shunters aren't the most exciting fare at Eastleigh Works. D2253 was a Drewry diesel-mechanical shunter of 1957. It managed to find employment for just 12 years before being scrapped by Cohen's of Kettering.

Below To conclude this section, Crewe North has provided something a bit more interesting in the form of 'Coronation' 'Pacific' No 46256, appropriately named after its eminent designer *Sir William A. Stanier FRS.* Beside it is 'Black Five' No 45311. Note the number of sewn-on badges on the duffel-bag!

6
SHED-BASHING

Steam sheds were never located at the best end of town, and my memories of arriving by coach at the end of a dingy cobbled cul-de-sac, or walking from the nearest station through streets of terraced houses, are perfectly evoked by this photograph of the back of Bolton shed in March 1968. The photographer's wife stands in Back Dobie Street (renamed locally 'Black Bogie Street') with the shed's coaling plant looming overhead and what looks like a Stanier loco beyond the fence.
Ray Ruffell, Silver Link Publishing collection

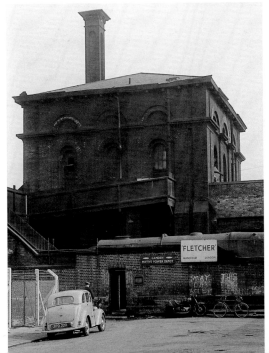

The entrance to Camden shed, north of Euston, was hardly imposing – just a door in the wall. The whole shed was on an extremely cramped site – as can be seen, a 'Princess Coronation' 'Pacific' is dropping down between the gate and the office entrance towards the ash plant.

The accompanying directions are from R. S. Grimsley's *The British Locomotive Shed Directory* of 1947. In his Preface the author writes, '...much precious time is often wasted in finding the way to locomotive sheds and works [and by using this book] enthusiasts may plan their valuable week-ends and holidays to the best advantage with the minimum of delay and trouble ... the shortest route being given except in a few cases where such a route would involve using a maze of back-streets and alleyways impossible to clearly describe.' *The late H. G. Forsyth, courtesy of Mrs M. M. Stratmann*

CAMDEN 1B.
The shed is on the west side of the main line about 1¼ miles north of Euston Station. The yard is visible from the line.
Cross the railway bridge (Regents Park Road) opposite Chalk Farm (L.P.T.B.) Station into Gloucester Road. Turn left into Dumpton Place, and the shed entrance is at the end of this short cul-de-sac. Walking time 5 minutes. See also under London.

NINE ELMS.
The shed is on a spur off the main L.S.W. line. The yard is not visible from the line.
Turn right outside Wandsworth Road Station along Wandsworth Road. Turn left into Brooklands Road. The shed entrance is at the end of this road. Walking time 15 minutes. See also under London.

Above Likewise, south of the river, what the entrance to Nine Elms lacked in grandeur and style it made up for in that wonderful sense of excitement and anticipation – what rarities will be on shed today? Three spotters from Wigan are making their way to the gate office on Saturday 13 May 1967. Despite two signs warning against trespassing and the broken-glass-topped walls, and while an official shed permit was always desirable, sheds could often be 'bunked' through a handy hole in the fence, and shed staff were more or less tolerant of bona fide enthusiasts. *Tom Heavyside, courtesy of John Stretton*

Below John Fenning's school party obviously has a permit, and what a feast of steam they are enjoying at Nine Elms in the early 1960s! *Rev John E. Fenning*

Above and below Having got used to seeing steam locos from a distance, or just 'from the waist up' at a station platform, only in the shed did one get a sense of the sheer *size* of the things! The young spotter, and indeed the older boys, are literally dwarfed by 'A4' No 60019 *Bittern*, more than 165 tons and 71 feet of engine and tender with driving wheels 6ft 8in in diameter. The shed is Perth (63A) in 1964. *Both David Hucknall*

Right Even the relatively modestly sized 126½-ton GWR 'Castles' had driving wheels of a similar diameter. Being on the wet oily floor of the shed beside those great wheels

and connecting rods was always an awesome experience! Happily the sight of No 7018 *Drysllwyn Castle* can still be enjoyed in preservation. *David Hucknall*

Above Some sheds and yards were little short of vast – Stratford in east London was one such. Mr Grimsley notes, 'The shed is in a maze of lines at the north-west side of the station... Note – This shed is the largest in the British Isles, and is very dispersed.' Some discussion appears to be taking place at 3.40pm on Friday 12 August 1955, perhaps prior to tackling the great expanse. Near at hand is ex-GER 'B12/3' 4-6-0 No 61556, which was withdrawn at Christmas 1957. *David Holmes*

Left Five years later, in October 1960, another knot of spotters has gathered, perhaps to discuss the loco beyond ex-LMS 2-6-0 No 46468. I had a particular affection for these 'Moguls' – for some years No 46495 was the yard shunter at Coventry, and could be heard moving to and fro from my school, which was almost next to, but out of sight of, the railway – very frustrating during long summer afternoon lessons when the windows were open and you longed to be out by the line! *John K. Morton, John Stretton collection*

Above Another large Southern Region shed with an extensive yard was Ashford, seen here during an RCTS visit in 1962. Much number-taking and photographing is taking place, and it is interesting to note the segregation between the veteran steam locos on the right and the newer Type 2 and 3 Bo-Bos on the left, which will only be a couple of years old. *Ken Fairey*

Below Much further west, but still on the Southern, Salisbury shed is being visited by an LCGB railtour on Sunday 3 April 1966. Virtually all the gentlemen have cameras, and are taking great interest in one of the last surviving 'N' Class 2-6-0s, No 31411, as well they might, for it was withdrawn from Stewarts Lane shed at the end of the month. Clinker, ash, firebars and discarded lamps form the usual shed yard detritus. *The late George Harrison, David Hucknall collection*

Above Another Southern-loco-hauled LCGB railtour visited Bath on Saturday 5 March 1966 to mark the passing of the much-loved Somerset & Dorset line, which was to be closed from the following Monday. The two locos in charge of the tour, Nos 34057 *Biggin Hill* and (behind it) 34006 *Bude*, are seen on Green Park Shed as the excursionists hurry forward to get a better look. The photograph was taken from the signal box, but then the privileged photographer was a railwayman! To compound the loss, neither 'Pacific' survived the cutter's torch. *Ray Ruffell, Silver Link Publishing collection*

Left Dorchester shed was similarly modest, and is seen here during a Thursday evening visit on 22 April 1954. Dorchester's own 'G6' 0-6-0T No 30162 takes centre stage, a typically handsome LSWR design by your compiler's namesake William Adams! *David Holmes*

Above In mac and flat cap, this mature spotter is noting the number of 285, a former Taff Vale Railway 0-6-2T, at Swindon on Saturday 23 February 1958. It is without its connecting rods, so is probably destined for scrap. *J. H. Bamsey, David Mitchell collection*

Below 'Castle' Class No 5038 *Morlais Castle* makes a fine sight on Oxford shed in the early 1960s, during a visit by the London Railfan Club. The 4-6-0 was withdrawn from Reading shed at the end of September 1963 and cut up the following summer. The photographer tells us that 'the fellow in the black jacket walking away from me is Roger Burfitt. He saw me at Bishops Lydeard in 2005 during a West Somerset Railway gala – only the second time that I'd seen him since leaving school in 1965.' *Richard Derry*

Above Railway works were also very popular for organised visits, and here a crocodile of enthusiasts young and old thread their way through the Erecting Shop at Crewe Works during an RCTS visit on Saturday 21 May 1966. *Ken Fairey*

Below Another string of spotters make their way up and down the lines of locos at Camden shed in the early 1960s during a school trip. Among the treasures on offer are No 46165 *The Ranger (12th London Regiment)* on the extreme left, No 46237 *City of Bristol* in the centre, and an unrebuilt 'Royal Scot' on the right – both the first two had gone before the end of 1964. Note the ash pit containing a small truck running on narrow-gauge tracks to take away the hot firebox ashes, while accumulated ash from the smokebox would be shovelled out into the trucks beside the track. *Rev John E. Fenning*

Above 'Satchels and flat caps at Newton Heath in the early 1960s' is how the photographer captions this photograph of a group of young spotters about to cab 0F 0-4-0T No 41532. These 'Deeley dock tanks' were a 1907 Midland Railway design, and eight survived at the end of the 1950s. *Chris Booth collection*

Below When this photograph first appeared in Silver Link's *Classic Steam: On Shed*, David Hucknall captioned it: 'With his gabardine raincoat (almost a uniform for the railway enthusiast of the period) sensibly belted, a trainspotter strolls past Worsdell 'J27' 0-6-0 No 65844, notebook in hand.' The scene is York shed on Saturday 2 May 1964. *David Hucknall*

Above Despite the potential for enormous noise, the interiors of steam sheds were often very quiet places, as the locomotives stood at rest either out of use or in light steam, just a gentle echoing hissing disturbing the peace. Surrounded by ex-Midland Railway locomotives, these spotters are using the central turntable of Derby's roundhouse shed to record the numbers ranged around them. The date is Saturday 11 May 1963, and the occasion a railtour from St Pancras to Derby, Buxton, Ashbourne, Burton-on-Trent, Leicester, and back to St Pancras. *Geoffrey Sheldon*

Below Never mind about sitting down for a drink – who could resist getting cracking on the wonderful array of locos in the yard at Bridlington shed on Thursday 7 August 1958? Most of the engines are ex-LNER machines, except for the 'Black Five' on the left, and at least three are carrying reporting numbers or headboards indicating that they have brought in excursions. *Mike Mitchell*

Above Enthusiasts were not just passive recorders of engine numbers – when special trains were running, some would turn out to make sure the loco concerned went out in a smarter and cleaner condition than might otherwise have been the case if left to the shed staff. At Nine Elms shed on Saturday 11 March 1967 two young girls in wellies get to work on the nameplate of preserved LNER 'K4' 2-6-0 No 3442 *The Great Marquess* prior to it working a railtour in Sussex and Hampshire. *Frank Hornby*

Above right Peter Fitton applies paint to the number of BR Standard 4MT 4-6-0 No 75041 at Blackpool Central shed on Sunday 27 September 1964; the occasion is not recorded. *Peter Fitton, John Stretton collection*

Below Enthusiasts Paul Riley and Paul Claxton are busy cleaning 'Jubilee' No 45647 *Sturdee* at Blackpool North

shed on Sunday 23 October 1966, ready to work a return special train to Leeds City. No doubt the famous Illuminations were the subject of the excursion – they finished on that day, having been switched on 52 nights earlier on 2 September by Ken Dodd. Eleven months later *Sturdee* was scrapped. *Peter Fitton, John Stretton collection*

7
OPEN DAYS

Above Shed or works open days or special exhibitions gave enthusiasts the opportunity to get closer to special locomotives – as these photographs show, *very* close in some cases! 'Under siege!' is how the photographer describes the state of preserved LSWR 'T9' 4-4-0 No 120 at Eastleigh Works Open Day on Wednesday 1 August

1962. The usual temporary steps have been provided to allow visitors to access the cab, but in those wild and reckless days before Health & Safety had been invented it seems that clambering all over the loco was OK too! *The late N. L. Browne, Frank Hornby collection*

Left At the station on the same day the assembled enthusiasts enjoy the sight of 9F 2-10-0 No 92129 running light – the loco is already half-way through its scandalously short 10-year life. *The late N. L. Browne, Frank Hornby collection*

Above In April 1961 British Railways held an exhibition of goods stock and locomotives in the goods yard at Marylebone. Among the exhibits was brand-new 'Deltic' No D9003, which had only been delivered to Finsbury Park on 27 March and was as yet without its *Meld* nameplates, which were applied at Doncaster in July. Behind it is new 'Warship' D865 *Zealous*. Peter Denton says, 'As I lived in Sheffield at the time, when visiting London it was always better and at that time quicker to travel from Sheffield Victoria down the much-lamented Great Central. I think we must have been in London for a football match and it just happened that the exhibition was being held in the goods yard. What I do recall is that we did not make the effort to get all the way to London just for the exhibition. For a Yorkshire lad to see anything from the GWR (the "Warship") was quite something.' *Peter H. Denton*

Below At the same exhibition was the iconic *Mallard*. No clambering all over the boiler at this show! *Peter H. Denton*

Above On Saturday 13 September 1958 the last surviving GNR Ivatt locos – 'J52' 0-6-0T No 68846 and 'C12' 4-4-2T No 67352 – were displayed at Noel Park at an exhibition to celebrate the 750th anniversary of the Borough of Wood Green. Both locos were beautifully presented by 'Top Shed' at King's Cross, but the 'C12' was completely unserviceable and had to be taken to the show by the 'J52', which, as Top Shed Pilot, was kept in good condition; in fact, the former GNR No 1247 went on to became the first BR locomotive to be bought privately for preservation, by Capt Bill Smith, in March the following year, as recounted in *1247: Preservation Pioneer* (Silver Link Publishing, 1991), and is now part of the National Collection. *Basil Coles*

Left Being able to officially 'cab' a loco was a great open day attraction. 'Brit' No 70035 *Rudyard Kipling* was completed just before Christmas 1952, and was on display in the bay platform at Ipswich in 1953 when these schoolboys got the chance to climb aboard; the photographer believes that the event had something to do with fund-raising for the victims of the severe flooding that had happened earlier that year. *David Buck*

So, back to locos 'under siege'. Unique 8P BR 'Pacific'
No 71000 *Duke of Gloucester* made a guest appearance at a
Derby Works open day in August 1960, and youngsters were

all over loco and tender like ants on a log. It was a wet day
and the paintwork was no doubt slippery, but no serious
injuries appear to have occurred... *All Geoffrey Sheldon*

Open Days are still very popular, but of course today have to be fully risk-assessed for Health & Safety. This is Crown Point, Norwich, on Saturday 24 September 1983, with steam and diesel locos old and new, together with rolling-stock and the ever-popular trade stands. *Roland Hummerston*

8 SPECIALS

Right Even well before the end of steam, the opportunity to travel behind a particular locomotive or over a rarely traversed or soon to be closed section of line was eagerly taken by enthusiasts. The latter is the occasion here, the penultimate day of services on the Wensleydale branch from Garsdale through Hawes to Northallerton. At 6.40pm on Saturday 24 April 1954 'J21' No 65038 of 1889, complete with wreath of flowers, prepares to leave the former Hawes Junction on the Settle & Carlisle line; the loco was withdrawn later in the year.
John Stretton collection

Below The Blagdon branch from Congresbury in Somerset lost its passenger service as long ago as 1931, but part of the branch remained open for freight until 1963. On Sunday 28 April 1957 the RCTS ran a tour along the branch behind ex-LMS 2-6-2T Nos 41202 and 41203, and it is seen here pausing at Wrington to allow the enthusiasts – typically smartly dressed – to alight and take photographs. The tie industry must have suffered dramatically reduced sales in more recent decades!
Mike Morant

Above The old Midland & South Western Railway route from Andoversford to Andover closed to passenger services from Monday 11 September 1961, and the day before the RCTS ran a special train along the line behind '4300' Class 2-6-0 No 5306. It has paused at Cirencester Watermoor station, and once again the passengers are exploring the site. Shirts, ties and sports jackets are as always much in evidence – the gentleman on the extreme left is wearing a bow-tie! *Alan Lillywhite, John Stretton collection*

Below The Blaenavon Low Level branch closed on 30 April 1962, and the following Sunday, 6 May, the last train along the branch was organised by the Midlands Area of the SLS. It is seen here at Blaenavon, with enthusiasts issuing from both sides of the train! The fashions are once again very characteristic of the age. *John Stretton collection*

Above The Purley-Caterham branch in Surrey opened on 5 August 1856, and its centenary was celebrated with special steam-hauled passenger trains, the first for many years. A 'Terrier' 0-6-0T and old 'birdcage' stock were used. *The late Prof H. P. White, Allan Mott collection*

Below The Caterham branch is still very much in use, but in Kent the idiosyncratic Hayling Island branch was closed with effect from Monday 4 November 1963. The branch was famous as one of the last stamping-grounds of the famous Stroudley 'Terrier' tanks, and No 32662 is at Havant at 2.35pm about to leave with the first special on the last day of services, Saturday 2 November – note the home-made laurel wreath. *Ray Ruffell, Silver Link Publishing collection*

On Saturday 12 May 1956 Ian Allan organised a 'Trains Illustrated Excursion', the 'Pennine Pullman', which began at Marylebone station behind No 60014 *Silver Link*. The 'A4' took the train to Sheffield, whence electric loco No 27002 *Aurora* took it to Guide Bridge. Former GCR 'Directors' Nos 62664 and 62662 then brought the train back to Sheffield via Rochdale and Barnsley, and *Silver Link* returned the happy enthusiasts to King's Cross. At 9.20am *Silver Link* was photographed at Marylebone. *Basil Coles*

The next year, on Wednesday 24 April 1957, an Ian Allan 'Plant Special' was taken from Paddington to Doncaster by sister 'A4' No 60029 *Woodcock*. On the return journey the loco failed at Nottingham Victoria with brake problems, and at just after 7 o'clock is seen being removed from the train by 'J39' No 64715, watched by a trio of no doubt disappointed enthusiasts. *Basil Coles*

Another railtour making a London departure is seen here on Saturday 19 September 1964. St Pancras's clock says exactly 8 o'clock, and a clutch of enthusiasts are getting their photographs of 'Royal Scot' No 46155 *The Lancer* at the head of the LCGB's 'Pennine Limited'. This was a last-chance opportunity, as the loco was withdrawn from Carlisle Kingmoor in December and scrapped. *Frank Hornby*

Above Steam from Waterloo ended on 9 July 1967, so in the months beforehand steam-hauled railtours were much in demand. On 4 July 1966 'Merchant Navy' No 35008 *Orient Line* waits to leave Waterloo with an unidentified special. The electrified lines mean that a policeman on one platform and a railway employee on the other are preventing the enthusiasts from indulging in their usual habit of off-platform swarming! *Orient Line* made it to the end, being withdrawn and scrapped a year later having achieved one of the highest mileages of the class, almost 1.3 million. *John Stretton collection*

Below The occasion is thought to be the LCGB's 'Vectis Farewell' railtour on New Year's Eve 1966 (steam on the Isle of Wight ended that year, and several lines were closed). On a dark, wet day the special, headed by Standard 5MT 4-6-0 No 73065 and another of the same class, waits to leave, while 'West Country' No 34002 *Salisbury* stands alongside with a service train. *Mike Morant*

Above Preserved North British Railway 4-4-0 No 256 *Glen Douglas* is at the terminus of the Langholm branch (off the Waverley route at Riddings) with the SLS 'Carlisle Railtour' of Saturday 6 April 1963. The following year the branch lost its passenger service, and closed completely in 1967. Enthusiasts of all ages are enjoying the event, including the gentleman in the centre with *two* cameras hanging from his neck. *Gavin Morrison*

Left At the other end of the country, the LSWR built five large and powerful 4-6-2 tanks to work the interchange traffic between Feltham and Brent/Willesden yards. No 30517 was disposed of on 31 December 1962, which is perhaps why it has been used to haul a special down the Chessington branch on Sunday 16 December. The midwinter sun highlights the loco (perhaps running round its train?) and the cameramen ranged up the bank to photograph it. *J. H. Bamsey, David Mitchell collection*

Right On a misty Sunday 17 October 1965 two preserved GWR tanks, 0-4-2T No 1420 and 0-6-0PT No 6435, stand at the up main platform at Ashchurch, north of Cheltenham, with an SLS special, framed by photographers. The Evesham branch diverges behind the enthusiasts on the right, and the Tewkesbury and Malvern line is off to the left. *Gerald Adams, John Stretton collection*

Below As the 1960s progressed, so the number of line closure specials increased. On Saturday 3 September 1966 the former Great Central London extension ceased to be a through route to the capital, being closed south of Rugby Central. On the last day of 'the last main line', 'B1' No 61173 is being prepared at Nottingham Victoria to take a railtour south. It was clearly a nice day for a sad occasion, as the shirt sleeves prove. The 'B1' was withdrawn from York the following January, and scrapped in March. *Roland Hummerston*

Above By the end of 1962 all the former Great Western 'King' Class had been withdrawn from service. No 6000 *King George V* was scheduled for preservation, while Nos 6023 and 6024, *King Edward II* and *King Edward I* respectively, were much later saved from the scrapyard and brought back to working order. On Sunday 28 April

1963, despite being on 'death row', No 6018 *King Henry VI* was sufficiently serviceable to be able to haul an SLS special, seen here being worshipped by the faithful at Southall. The loco was finally cut up at the end of September. *J. H. Bamsey, David Mitchell collection*

Left No 7029 *Clun Castle* was built by BR at Swindon as late as May 1950; it was the last 'Castle' to remain in BR service and was withdrawn at the end of 1965 for preservation. Prior to withdrawal it achieved its finest moment at the head of an enthusiasts' special on Saturday 27 November 1965 commemorating the end of express steam working on the Western Region. On the descent of Wellington bank in Somerset No 7029 achieved a top speed of 96mph on the fastest ever recorded timing over the arduous route from Plymouth to Bristol. The loco hauled the last steam service train from Paddington in 1965 and was also the last steam engine to leave the former Snow Hill station with a passenger train. The 'Farewell to Steam' railtour is seen here, appropriately, at Swindon. *J. H. Bamsey, David Mitchell collection*

Right The end for steam age spotters and enthusiasts came in August 1968, and many specials were organised to mark the sad occasion. On Sunday 4 August, the last 'regular' weekend prior to BR's final steam-hauled railtour, the RCTS ran an 'End of Steam Commemorative Railtour' from London to Manchester and a circuit of northern lines. Unfortunately, the tour suffered severe delays; booked to arrive at Blackburn just before 2pm, by then it was running 170 minutes late. Not that any of the assembled enthusiasts seem to mind, as 8F 2-8-0 No 48476 is taken from the train and replaced by 'Black Five' No 45407, leading Standard 4-6-0 No 73069. The locomotive change over-ran the allotted time, and the tour had to be curtailed. Even so, final arrival back at Euston was still some 270 minutes late! *Roland Hummerston*

Below 'The ground at Rainhill exhibited a very lively appearance; several thousand persons were collected from all parts of the country ... in short, the *tout ensemble* exhibited as much bustle and excitement as if the great St Leger had been about to be contested.' That was a contemporary account of the famous Rainhill locomotive trials on the Liverpool & Manchester Railway, which commenced on Tuesday 6 October 1829. Just short of 139 years later, on Sunday 11 August 1968, the legendary 'Fifteen Guinea Special' paused for a 'photo opportunity'. This 315-mile, almost 11-hour journey marked the end of standard gauge steam-hauled passenger services on British Railways, and was billed as the 'Last steam-hauled train on British Railways on standard gauge track'. It's just after 9.30am and 'Black Five' No 45110 has brought the train from Liverpool Lime Street en route to Manchester. *Roger Siviter ARPS*

'Britannia' 'Pacific' No 70013 *Oliver Cromwell* took over at Manchester and took the special to Bolton, Blackburn and Hellifield, then via the Settle & Carlisle line to Carlisle. It's now 2.30pm, and with cars filling the moorland road as far as the eye can see, and enthusiasts 'invading the pitch', the special pauses at Ais Gill. There have been many steam-hauled trains passing this way since, of course, but it terms of everyday BR steam this was The End. *Roger Siviter ARPS*

9

CAMERAMEN

In the early days railway photography was not for everyone – the equipment was cumbersome and the processing expensive. As Michael Baker explains in his excellent book *Taking The Train* (Patrick Stephens Ltd, 1993), it became possible to take pictures of fast moving objects at the end of the 1880s. By the turn of the century photographs were usually of stationary or distant trains, but 10 years later close-up shots of moving trains were becoming more competent, and published railway photographs began to be credited to the individuals who had taken them. By the late 1950s the telephoto lens and the relative cheapness and excellent quality of Japanese-made single-lens reflex cameras encouraged more and more enthusiasts to take up the hobby, and look at railways in a more creative way, leading to the so-called 'New Wave' era of the 1960s. Today digital technology means that most photographers can easily equip themselves with a pocket-sized camera, and few will be seen without one. Back in early 1962, the date of this advert, the Coronet 6x6, at £3 10s 11d – then a quarter of the average weekly wage, or about £125 today – gave '12 big pictures'. For the same money, or a lot less, one can now get several hundred digital pictures in full colour with no processing costs!

On Saturday 2 June 1962 it's not possible to tell if either of these photographers at Newcastle-upon-Tyne is using a Coronet – the nearer gentleman is carrying a large case – but the worthy object of their precious pictures is 'A1' 4-6-2 No 60144 *King's Courier*, arriving with the 9.05am King's Cross-Tyne Commissioners Quay train. The 'Pacific' is being detached, no doubt for replacement by a smaller loco for the final part of the journey.
Michael Mensing

123

Left Going for the low-angle shot is this photographer at Waterloo on Friday 29 May 1966, and the loco is 'West Country' 'Pacific' No 34100 *Appledore*. *J. H. Bamsey, David Mitchell collection*

Left The snapper snapped! 'Castle' Class No 5069 *Isambard Kingdom Brunel* stands at Bristol Bath Road shed. While Brunel was building the Great Western Railway, French photographic pioneer Louis Daguerre was developing the process named after him, and in the year the GWR opened as far as Maidenhead, William Fox Talbot in England succeeded in making photographic prints on silver chloride paper. *David Hucknall*

Below A trio of photographs capture *Flying Scotsman* arriving at Doncaster with an Aberdeen-Waterloo special, carrying 'The Aberdonian' headboard, on Sunday 26 June 1966. *Peter Fitton, John Stretton collection*

Above Many great names have been associated with railway photography, and one of the best-known over the last 50 years has been Brian Morrison, who used his National Service demob money to buy a camera for railway photography. Now a freelance author and photographer, he has written more than 25 books and has taken tens of thousands of photographs. At Wigan Central shed on Friday 26 August 1955 he is 'the young-looking bespectacled spotter/photographer' (his words) walking away from ex-LMS 2P 4-4-0 No 40680.
Roy E. Wilson, Brian Morrison collection

Right Brian was the consultant for Michael Baker's aforementioned book about railway photographers, *Taking the Train*, and this shot was set up as a possible cover picture. Although the ambience is definitely 1950s – 'Q1' 0-6-0, vintage tripod, and Brian in overcoat and 'pork-pie' hat – the picture was actually taken near Sheffield Park on the Bluebell Railway in 1992. *Michael Baker*

Above Forming a pleasing arc along the platform at Manchester Victoria on Saturday 1 June 1968, four photographers capture Stanier 8F No 48168 as it waits during banking duties for the climb to Miles Platting. A few months later such everyday sights would only exist on film.
Roger Siviter ARPS

Left Thirty-six years later, on 16 September 2004, a more recent freight engine, No 67028, is photographed from the platform at Wareham station, returning from hauling a train of empty gas tanks to Furzebrook on the former Swanage branch. Built in Spain under contract from the American company General Motors – what would Sir William Stanier have said about that…?
Michael Baker

Above Railway recording *par excellence*: John Spencer Gilks is ready with his cameras, microphone and tape-recorder at Crofton Curve near Savernake on 3 June 1962, the day after the first photograph in this chapter was taken. *Allan Lillywhite*

Below A quarter of a century later bulky equipment has not entirely been eliminated. Tripods are set up and focuses adjusted at Waterloo station on 'Network Day' in 1987. *Allan Mott*

Below right Even though steam has long gone, steam age railway infrastructure is still to be seen, although less and less survives with the passing years. Having deliberately set out to record photographically the pre-electrification, semaphore-signalled Midland main line, David Stonor, Keith Bell and John Gilks determined to make a similar pilgrimage to the Great Western between London and Reading. Here David and Keith capture the scene at Iver on 16 September 1978. *John Spencer Gilks*

INDEX OF LOCATIONS